SURRENDER

Your Key to Spiritual Success

Arthur Burt

D0061727

CREATION
HOUSE
ORLANDO, FLORIDA

Creation House
Strang Communications Company
600 Rinehart Road
Lake Mary, FL 32746
(407) 333-3132 • Fax: (407) 333-7100
Web site: http://www.creationhouse.com

Material contained in this document was originally
published in two separate works entitled *Boomerang:
The Funeral of Failure* and *The Lost Key.*

Unless otherwise noted, all Scripture quotations
are from the King James Version of the Bible.

Scripture quotations marked AMP are from the
Amplified Bible. Old Testament copyright © 1965, 1987
by the Zondervan Corporation. The Amplified
New Testament copyright © 1954, 1958, 1987 by
the Lockman Foundation. Used by permission.

*Dedicated to those who missed the bus
but who got there just the same
because someone gave them a lift.*

*God does much with little,
most with least and
everything with nothing.*

ACKNOWLEDGMENT

Much time and effort is needed to complete a book. Special acknowledgment is due to Maureen Eha for her tireless and capable work in bringing this project into reality. Without her selfless contribution this book would have remained but a thought. For many hours she wrote, edited and transcribed recent messages to capture Arthur Burt's personality and teaching on paper. Now others who are unable to hear him in person can read, benefit from and be impacted by his message.

CONTENTS

FOREWORD

There have been many waves of the Spirit of God throughout the centuries as truth which had been abandoned over time was restored to the church. Beginning in the 1500s there were identifiable waves of reformation, and they have continued until now. In this century the pace seems to have increased as we have experienced the Pentecostal outpouring, the healing revivals, the Latter Rain movement, the charismatic renewal and more.

Unfortunately, the waves of spiritual renewal were usually followed by an ebb that resulted in a variety of clutter littering the spiritual landscape. The litter usually included human moral failure, doctrinal error, and more fractures and factions in the church. Spiritual unction turned to form.

No matter what the end result, the process to failure begins the same way. But the Scripture gives us ways to avoid or return from failure and embrace God's grace as strength. It teaches us to deal with the cause of failure rather than the effect.

As the signs of a fresh move of the Holy Spirit are evident today, it is particularly relevant to see what can prevent the current move from ending in failure as have many in the past. A move of God is really a personal thing—renewing one person at a time. Only as the individual reviving becomes widespread does it become recognized as "revival."

Arthur Burt is a prophet who speaks a word that is for the times. He preaches a message, backed by the radical life he has lived, which calls us to abandon the lesser realm and soar with the eagles in the Spirit. He has had a major impact on my life as he has on many others around the world.

Parts of this book were previously published as booklets in the 1970s under the names *The Lost Key* and *Boomerang: The Funeral of Failure.* Those teachings as well as messages from his current ministry were combined in this book. His message presents an antidote for failure and the key for long-term spiritual success. It is possible to find the key to stay in God's plan and presence and not end up as spiritual debris at the end of a move of the Spirit.

As you read this book, ask the Holy Spirit to speak to you and show you how to use the key in your own life. Then you can witness "the funeral of failure."

Joy Strang
Lake Mary, Florida
March, 1997

What claim can this little book make
as it joins the millions of other books
that vie like raucous street vendors
for the eye and ear of
a fleeting fickle public?

To life there are many keys
but only *one* master key!

What is it?

Where is it?

This unpretentious little book
claims to declare it!

ONE

THE LOST KEY

Have you ever given your spouse the only set of keys to the house or car? If you have, then you can identify with one of the characters in the following drama.

Wife, digging through her purse: "I can't find the key!"

Husband, growing impatient: "You *what?*"

Wife: "*I can't find the key!*"

Husband: "Well, where did you put it?

Wife: "Oh, don't be silly! If I knew where I put it, I wouldn't be looking for it, now, would I?"

How many times have you participated in such a

conversation? In how many different scenarios? Fumbling fingers in the pale moonlight! Shivering figures on the front door step! Tired travelers by the curbside with a cozy car, so near and yet so far, that defies all efforts to enter!

What is this elusive object that we have so much trouble hanging onto?

The key!

We seek it here, we seek it there, we seek it everywhere! Why is it so important? What does it do?

It locks the door, starts the engine, allows me to enter my own home, prevents the stranger access to private territory, turns a door into a barrier, imprisons a man for life or, with one flick of a finger, allows me to leave rain, cold, storm and dark for warmth, comfort, light and friendship. So small but so vital! I may be only a hundred miles from my destination and in possession of a machine that can eat up the miles, but without a key to enter or start the engine, it is almost impossible to get where I want to go.

Obviously, the key is an essential object.

We use the word *key* in a variety of expressions: Gibraltar, the *key* to the Mediterranean; the code, the *key* to decipher the meaningless message; the *key* man; the *key* word; the *key* job!

Does God Have a Key?

Does God have a key? If so, what is it? What is it for?

So many people are in prison with no key to the solution that would set them free! The *inward* prison and the inward chains are a thousand times worse than any *concrete* prison's black despair; they produce a more hopeless helplessness than ever the barebacked galley slaves experienced when they were chained in rows by ankles and wrists, their cruel taskmasters lashing their bleeding backs as their oars dipped in perfect unison to cut swiftly through the gleaming waters. No blacksmith can forge, no key cutter fashion, a key to open the dungeon of utter numbness that is the experience of millions who are in bondage to deadly, vicious habits and fear.

Pile up all your worldly solutions: Psychiatry, drugs, amusement parks, night clubs, bingo halls, pep talks and weekend get-aways; then stand back and take a good look. None of these will ever meet man's deepest need and set him free from his failure and his sin! Is there a key to unlock the inward prison?

Consider the man who is consumed by a lust for money, power or women and has made a shambles of his life by pursuing something other than God's will for him; who has exchanged ethics for greed and humility for self-aggrandizement; who has settled for living a lie rather than dwelling in the truth. Is there a key that will turn his failure into success?

What is it? *Where* is it? I spent many years of my life looking for it, without knowing what I was seeking. Over and over again I came up against failure in different areas of my life, until God finally revealed to me the cause of my failure and the key to turning it around.

The key that I was looking for was originally lost in the garden of Eden. God can identify with the spouse who gave away his only set of keys! He once gave a very important key to Adam and Eve, but they lost it in the paradise He had created for them. When they did, they placed the rest of us in a position for failure and set us on a search to find the way out of it.

We are left, like the couple we met earlier, in a fix:

"I can't find the key!"

"Well, where did you put it?"

"Oh, don't be silly! If I knew where I put it, I wouldn't be looking for it, now, would I? In fact, *I'm not sure I've ever had it!*"

If you can identify with this experience, if you are

wondering where to find the key that will release you or someone you know from the bondage of sin and the frustration of failure, read on. Perhaps you can also identify with one of the real-life examples of failure that I discuss in the next chapter.

TWO

FAILURE: TRUTH'S APPRENTICESHIP

As of the year of publication for this book (1997), I have been a Christian for seventy years. I have seen a lot of failure, not just in my own life but in many lives. I have ministered to many failures. I have sat where they have sat. Is a doctor qualified to practice who has not been sick? Even Jesus was in all points tempted!

I have experienced failure in many areas: emotional, physical and financial. My own marriage could have dissolved right at the outset, because I was involved with a woman who was not my wife for seven years. I made all sorts of resolutions, tried and cried, ran away from the situation, vowed and declared, gave her up again and again—but failed!

Emotional Failure

I played about with the affections of a schoolgirl from the time she was twelve until she was nearly sixteen. Only God got me out; I couldn't save myself. I failed!

Here is what happened. I was always fond of children. The kids knew me as "Uncle Arthur," and many were the games and conjuring tricks we shared. Among the children was a young girl who became attached to our family and who would come up to the house to help my wife with the children by taking the baby out and so on. She did this for years. Time passed; she was ten, eleven, twelve, thirteen years old.

One Christmastime we were having some fun and games, and I kissed her! She put her arm at the back of my neck and held me tight. I immediately noticed her response (I suppose it fed my pride), and from that moment on, I paid a lot more attention to her. We engaged in the surreptitious cuddle when my wife was out of the room, the "scuffle" for a handkerchief or what-have-you which allows hands to wander where they shouldn't, and other forms of inappropriate behavior. Eventually our playing around developed into a little "affair." By this time, the girl was almost sixteen.

There were "accidental" meetings on purpose, excuses that gave us the opportunity to be alone. I found ways for her to help me with "work" I had to do. It was no longer enough to see her when she came to help my wife at home. I began to meet her in the woods. I was too "spiritual" to go the ultimate in the affair and too carnal to leave her alone and not trifle with her affections. I would fondle her flesh while I "ministered" to her spirit; so what grace should do, my pride became a substitute for.

One day another brother (a fellow minister in the meetings we were having at a local mission) approached me about this situation. He said that the young girl's mother had asked him to speak to me and request that I leave the girl alone. She was not eating or sleeping, and her mother believed that the child's unhealthy state was due to her infatuation for me.

I glared at him! Outwardly I was calm, but on the inside I was blazing. I thought, "You, you speak to me about this; I'm lily white compared to you!" I knew he was involved in an affair up to his neck. His marriage was a shambles. His wife spent night after night at our house telling her troubles to us. More than once I had steered her away from suicide and maybe even murder (crockery smashed and blows struck had been the order of the day and night at their house). That was only one situation in his life—by no means the only one! So I rejected the word because of the vessel: a very dangerous response.

Perfection isn't in the appointed one; it is in the appointment. If the postman's trousers are muddy, that is no excuse for rejecting the letter he hands me! I had no right to refuse the message simply because I didn't like the carrier. But I was furious inside, and the more I brooded on the life of the brother who had confronted me, the more I judged.

The next night, because one of our children was not well, my wife stayed home, and I went to the meeting on my bicycle (during the war years and for some time after, we were able to get gas only with a permit). I took my little girl on a chair at the back. After the meeting I walked part of the way home with the young woman I had grown close to, sharing what had happened. At the top of the hill I bade her good night, mounted my bicycle with my little girl at the back and rode down the hill.

Blackout still prevailed in England as a result of the war; there were no lights. The only light I had came from a dynamo on the back wheel of the bicycle. Whenever the wheel stopped, the light went out. At the bottom of the hill the road led through a pitch-black vale of trees, beyond which, about a mile further on, I lived. With not another vehicle in sight and no other source of light besides that on the wheel, I swept down the steep hill. At the bottom of it, where the road bore left, I leaned over to the left. By this time I was traveling at nearly top speed. There was a shattering, shuddering screech as the back wheel buckled, almost throwing me. The light went out; my little girl began screaming; and there was not another soul or light around!

I put my hand to the back in the dark and felt something warm and wet. I knew what it was—my little girl's blood! Her leg was trapped in the buckled wheel! Somehow I managed to get my leg over the handlebars and, lifting the whole weight on the buckled back wheel, "frog-marched" the bike to a wall in the pitch-black darkness. There I frenziedly tried to pull the bicycle spokes out of her flesh as she bled and screamed. They seemed to be embedded to the bone. *Oh, God,* I thought, *if only I had a light!* But there was no light and no help.

Finally, in despair, I gave up the struggle and, taking the whole weight, I rolled my screaming child uphill in the dark, on the front wheel. It seemed like a thousand miles! Once we were home and in the light, my wife and I eventually got our child free from the spokes. We prayed and bathed, bathed and prayed. I decided to trust God to heal her.

That night—a sleepless one—little fingers pushed through the crib rails and clutched Daddy's hand, as my little girl sobbed and I tried to comfort her. It was seven weeks before I knew whether or not she was going to walk.

All the time God was speaking to me. I learned the difference between pride and sin! I learned that God would forgive me for my failure, wrong as it might be, but that

He would never forgive the pride which made me rise up against my brother. "God resisteth the proud" (1 Pet. 5:5).

The next trip to the seaside I arranged for the girl whose affections I had toyed with to sit by a particular young man on the train. The two of them hit it off right away. They have been married for forty-three years or more now and have three grown sons.

Physical and Financial Failure

I have suffered physical as well as emotional failure. In my early thirties I had heart trouble, brought on by nothing but my pride. In those days, starting handles were used to crank car engines, and I would show off out in the cold weather by cranking heavy Chevrolet engines. If others couldn't, I could! I paid the price! I became so weak I couldn't hold a newspaper out at arm's length. The bedclothes felt like a ton weight as I gasped to breathe. I had stabbing pains in my heart. If I had to stand, I leaned against the wall. I couldn't use a paint brush or a spade or do any work at all with my arm. I was a physical failure!

I have also known financial failure. I've rubbed shoulders with poverty. When money failed in the mining area in which we lived, I dragged a tin bathtub on wheels around the back lanes to transport the "brass knockers," or coal with stone in it, that I picked up for our fire. I did this for years.

During the war I had an income of only forty shillings (about five dollars) for myself, my wife, one child and another relative to live on: four shillings for tithe, eight shillings for rent, five shillings for clinic and baby food, and five shillings for a widowed mother without a pension, leaving a grand total of eighteen shillings for the remainder of our expenses. I proved God in those days! I had to! The hard times I endured gave new meaning to Jesus' words, "Gather up the fragments...that nothing be lost" (John 6:12).

I knew even more severe deprivation during World War II when Hitler was only the width of the English Channel away. There was nothing in the shops, all supplies were depleted, and I ended up in prison because of what I believed. My inability to minister as God had called me to, my separation from my family, and the humiliating circumstances I faced at this time were almost more than I could bear.

You Can Make Lemonade from Your Lemons

As my experiences have proved, failure is a part of life; it is truth's apprenticeship for us. We don't have to roll in the mud to know it's black, but most of us start this way! We are like the person who once said, "Everything I like is either immoral, illegal or fattening!" In his letter to the Romans, the Apostle Paul echoes this sentiment: "The good that I would I do not: but the evil which I would not, that I do" (Rom. 7:19).

I understand what Paul is saying. For twenty-five years I tried, like a good Christian, to carry out the teaching of the Sermon on the Mount and found I couldn't do it; I failed! I gave it up in disgust and decided to leave the Sermon on the Mount up the mount! It was some years later before I discovered that the Christian life isn't hard to live; it's impossible to live, and only Jesus can live it. Then I recognized that my only struggle was the struggle not to struggle: to let go and let God!

In other words, I learned from my failure. I came to understand that the seed of success lies in what appears to be merely a mass of pulp. There is no such thing as waste with God! Waste is a lack of revelation. *Dung* may not be a nice word, but it is a wonderful fertilizer!

Failure is an essential ingredient in the recipe for success. It *is* possible for me to make lemonade from my

Failure: Truth's Apprenticeship

lemons instead of letting them turn me sour! Knowing this helps to take the sting of fear out of failure.

From Failure to Success

Let's consider a Biblical example. When Jesus was about to be crucified, Peter denied Him three times (see John 18:17,25,27). And he did this after insisting that he was willing to lay down his life for Jesus' sake (John 13:37). But Peter's apparent failure did not prevent him from successfully fulfilling God's purpose for his life; in fact, on the day of Pentecost, he preached out of his experience on the very topic which had caused his shame: denial. "Ye have denied the holy One!" he accused the Jews (see Acts 2:22-23,36).

Samson was also a failure at one time in his life. When he told Delilah the secret of his strength, he betrayed God and allowed the Philistines to take God's chosen vessel for routing His enemies (that is, Samson himself) out of commission. But the Bible tells us that Samson later redeemed himself, for "The dead [Philistines] which he slew at his death were more than they which he slew in his life" (Judg. 16:30).

The lives of Peter and Samson exemplify the truth that failing does not constitute failure in a life that is dedicated to God. Failing may have the appearance of a beast, but appearance is only skin deep. Underneath its ugly countenance is a prince. If our attitude toward failure is the appropriate one (and we shall see later what this is), God will turn our failure into success.

Remember: He always wins who sides with God! To him no chance is lost. Jesus told Peter, "Satan hath desired to have you, that he may sift you as wheat" (Luke 22:31). But when Satan sifts, God separates—the wheat from the chaff! We are better conformed to His image after our failure than before. God uses the devil for His own purposes! Jesus knew that Peter would be stronger

19

after his denial; He encouraged him, saying, "When thou art converted, strengthen thy brethren" (v. 32).

So Peter, the failure, ministered on denying. And Samson, the failure, destroyed more of God's enemies after his haircut than before. Out of their "deaths" came forth life, not to the glory of Peter or Samson, but to the glory of God. Jesus said, "Except a corn of wheat fall into the ground and die, it abideth alone: but if it die, it bringeth forth much fruit" (John 12:24). *If it dies, it multiplies!*

Death by fire produces ashes, and God gives beauty for ashes (Is. 61:3). He promises to restore the wasted years, the years the enemy has stolen from us while we dwelt in a place of failure (Joel 2:25). He says, in essence, "I will give you back again." More than once He declares, "My people shall *never* be ashamed" (vv. 26-27, italics added). When we have gone through the fire, we can no longer be burned! Ashes are an end product!

God brings life from death, beauty from ashes, success from failure. How?

To Have Success, We Must Have Truth

In order for God to bring about success from our failure, the failure must be attended by the truth. If the truth is that "the truth shall make [one] free," then no man is going to get *out* of his failure until he has had the truth *about* his failure! (John 8:32). I have to *own* where I am before I can *disown* where I am!

Most of us want to cover up our mistakes or deny that we have missed God on an issue. But receiving the truth means acknowledging our sins and accepting the blame for our failures. First John 1:8 says, "If we say that we have no sin, we deceive ourselves, and *the truth is not in us*" (italics added). On the other hand, "If we confess our sins, [God] is faithful and just to forgive us our sins, and to cleanse us from all unrighteousness" (v. 9). Thus an attitude of humility puts us in line to obtain the mercy and grace of God for our sins.

The problem is that sin is a consequence, not a cause. We cannot get rid of sin by dealing with sin. We must get at the root, or the cause, of it. You will never eliminate cobwebs by dusting cobwebs down; you must catch the spider! Many plants bush out when you cut only the top off. No wonder John the Baptist said, "The axe is laid into the *root* of the trees" (Matt. 3:10, italics added).

If sin is only the cobweb, then what is the spider? And what is the key for catching it? Or, how do we get at the root of the tree?

THREE

THE DEVIL MADE ME DO IT

Most of us laugh when we hear someone say, "The devil made me do it!" as an excuse for sin. But unfortunately, the belief that Satan is the cause of personal failure is all too common. Many unbelieving believers magnify his power. They insist that he is the root of all their problems. Those who want to escape responsibility find a convenient scapegoat in the devil and do not hesitate to put all the blame on his broad back.

They are like the newly-arrived Irish labourer who said on the building site, "Pwhat ivver it is, O'm again it!" Just as some citizens blame the government for everything, many Christians blame the devil for everything.

Is the devil to blame? Jesus did say of the woman with a spirit of infirmity, "*Satan* hath bound [this woman], lo, these eighteen years" (Luke 13:16, italics added). And the Scriptures do admonish us, "Resist the devil"; "Be sober, be vigilant...your adversary the devil, as a roaring lion, walketh about, seeking whom he may devour"; and "Put on the whole armour of God, that ye may be able to stand against the wiles of the devil" (James 4:7; 1 Pet. 4:8; Eph. 6:11). Further, they declare, "We wrestle not against flesh and blood, but against principalities, against powers, against the rulers of the darkness of this world" (Eph. 6:12).

Are we the helpless pawns of a raging, mighty despot who has sent our God reeling back? Is this the ninth round in a ten-round contest in which our God, bruised and bleeding, is despairingly looking to us, His seconds, to revive Him for a last-minute knockout?

What You Believe Rules You

Is this the picture? *Is* it? Is this the concept you have of God? What you believe rules you! The attitude of many Christians is one of blank negativism: They have a great big devil and a tiny little Saviour! Fear governs their lives. They see devils on the mantlepiece and demons on the bedposts in spite of God's Word, which declares, "Thou shalt *not* be afraid" and "God hath not given us the spirit of fear; but of power, and of love, and of a sound mind" (Ps. 91:5, italics added; 2 Tim. 1:7).

Such Christians encourage, by their negative thinking, a God-dishonoring fear. They act as if they catch demons like dirty people catch fleas, with spirits hopping from one to another as a result of physical contact. They have no positive faith whatsoever! They belie the truth of what someone has said, "There is not one negative note in the New Testament after Jesus rose from the dead. Hallelujah!"

"If God be for us, who can be against us?" (Rom. 8:31). *His* is the kingdom; *His* is the power; and *His* is the glory! (See Matt. 6:13.)

God is not running around His universe like a scalded cat, calling for volunteers to help Him defeat the devil! The devil is not *going* to be defeated; he *is* defeated!

That is what Calvary is all about. What else does Calvary mean? The term *spoiled* in Col. 2:15 is past tense regarding principalities and powers; the phrase *hath put* in Eph. 1:22 leaves no doubt about *all* things being under the feet of Jesus. When God *puts*, He is the greatest Put-er in the universe, and when *He* puts, things *stay* put!

We are not *going* to win! We *have* won! When Jesus died, His last words were not, "To be continued". They were, "It is finished" (John 19:30). He said what He meant. He meant what He said. Right believing produces right living, just as wrong believing produces wrong living. "Be ye transformed by the re*new*ing of your *mind*" (Rom. 12:2, italics added).

We need to remember two things: (1) The devil is defeated *now!* (2) We *have* won! (See Rom. 8:2.) The law of the Spirit of life in Christ Jesus not *will* make me free but *hath* made me free!

Why Did God Make the Devil?

If your experience does not tally with God's Word, scrap it and find a new one. Satan is a creature and not the Creator. You ask, "If God has all power, why doesn't He kill the devil?" Surely a reasonable enough question! Or, "If God knew the end from the beginning, why did He ever make the devil?" The answer to this second question has three parts.

First, God does not *make* devils; He did not *make* Satan a devil.

Second, the divine plan was to make responsible creatures of choice (those who have the power to choose). You can't choose with less than two! You can't choose the way of life unless there is a way of death, the narrow way unless there is a broad way, God unless there is a devil!

Third, God made a responsible creature of choice who *became* the devil! This is important. We must not charge the All Wise with folly! Satan, heaven's prime minister according to many scriptures (Ezek. 28:13-19 and others), plotted treason, took glory, exalted himself and was cast out of heaven as lightning. God did know the end from the beginning and declared it (Is. 46:10). He knew all along what the devil would be! He *permitted* him to become what he is.

A strong man defeats his enemy; a wise man uses his enemy. God is both strong and wise. So then: The devil is not the basis of man's failure; rather, he is God's sheepdog to drive the wandering sheep back to the Shepherd. He is a secondary, and not a primary, cause of sin.

In the book of Job Satan said to God, acknowledging Him as the Source of all power, "Hast not thou made an hedge about [Job]?...But put forth thine hand now, and touch all that he hath, and he will curse thee to thy face" (Job 1:10-11). Then God said to Satan, "Behold, all that [Job] hath is in thy power" (Job 1:12). Obviously it was not until Satan got his permit from headquarters that he was allowed to attack Job. Notice, too, that it was a limited permit: "Upon [Job] *himself* put not forth thine hand" (Job 1:12, italics added).

What Power Does the Devil Have?

Jesus declared, "All power is given unto me in heaven and in earth" (Matt. 28:18). Is this true? If it is, how much power has the devil got?

The power of the devil is a permitted power to deceive (those who choose to be deceived) by making God a liar. Nothing else, nothing more. Satan is essential to the divine purpose of choice!

The will of God is that man should choose, but *not* that he should be made (robot-like) to choose God, thereby eliminating the responsibility of choice. God said to Pharaoh, "For this cause have I raised thee up, for to show *in thee* [not just around thee] my power; and *that my name may be declared throughout all the earth*" (Ex. 9:16, italics added).

The power of choice was given only to man, not to cabbages and turnips, rats and rabbits or even mountains, oceans, sun, moon and stars. When God decrees, "An oak tree shall grow there," the tree does not have the power to say, "No, I won't," or to decide that it will become a stick of rhubarb instead. Only of mankind is it said that "as many as received him, to them gave he power to become the *sons of God*" (John 1:12, italics added).

Man has the power of choice: the power to change from one to the other! But what power does the devil have? As Jesus said of Pilate, so may we say of Satan, "Thou couldest have *no power* at all against me, *except it were given thee from above*" (John 19:11, italics added).

Ultimately, the devil can do nothing that God does not allow him to do. And what he intends for evil, God uses for our good (Rom. 8:28). Thus, Satan is not the spider, and therefore, eliminating him (supposing we could) is not the key to turning failure into success.

FOUR

SOME KEYS, BUT NOT *THE* KEY

A man who had experienced many storms in his marriage was asked, after all attempts at reconciliation had failed, "Have you ever considered divorce?" "Divorce?" he replied incredulously. "No, never! But murder, yes, hundreds of times!"

This little anecdote exemplifies the truth that there is usually more than one possible solution to a problem.

If Not Satan, Then What?

If, as I stated at the end of the last chapter, Satan is

not the spider—the cause of sin and failure—then eliminating him is not the key we are looking for. So what is?

Some may say that it is religion, yet a thousand voices challenge the validity of such an answer as they cry of religious people, "We cannot hear what you *say* for the noise of what you *are!*"

Next in the angling queue on life's pier is the Christian seeking to obey the words of Jesus: "Follow me, and I will make you fishers of men" (Matt. 4:19). This Christian produces not a hook but a net. He declares, "Religion is not the key, but Christ is the answer!"

The Christian certainly is right, but the wily, worldly-wise "fish" does not swim into the net. He does not read the Bible, but he does read Christians, so he politely or impolitely declines the bait. Why? Could the answer lie in the sarcastic slur, "See how these Christians *love* one another"? Do our divisions and lack of love and unity preach more eloquently than all our preachers?

Going into a church no more makes a man a Christian than going into a garage would make him a motor car. "Ye *must* be born again" (John 3:7, italics added).

After all, *being* is more important than *saying*, although what you *say* takes its authority from what you *are! The Lord bless me and my wife, our John and his wife, us four and no more, Amen.* Are we too inwardly focused? Certainly one could well say that love is *a* "lost" key if it is not *the* lost key! The following hymn points out the uselessness of the trappings of Christianity (church buildings, fancy organs, painted and sculpted images of Jesus) without love.

Said Christ the Lord, "I will go and see,
How the men, my brethren, believe in Me."
Great organs surged through arches dim,
Their jubilant floods in praise of Him,

28

And in church and palace and judgment hall,
He saw His image high over all.
But still, wherever His steps they led
The Son of God bent down His head!
Then Christ sought out an artisan,
A low-browed, stunted, haggard man,
And a motherless girl with fingers thin,
Who pushed from her, faintly, want and sin.
There set He in the midst of them,
And as they drew back their garments' hem
For fear of defilement,
"Lo, these," said He,
"Are the images ye have made of Me!"

This hymn is a commentary on the words of James 2:15-16: "If a brother or sister be naked, and destitute of daily food, And one of you say unto them, Depart in peace, be ye warmed and filled; notwithstanding ye give them not those things which are needful to the body; what doth it profit?" What good are the cathedrals, the organs, and the stained glass windows without love?

It would be better to go out into the streets and minister to the practical needs of the homeless one time than to spend every Sunday warming a pew in a fancy church when your heart is not right. Actions speak louder than words.

Is Deliverance the Key?

There is another apparent remedy for failure besides Satan, religion, pseudo-Christianity and love: outward deliverance. To employ this remedy, we suppress, or smother, or cover up what is wrong on the inside so that outwardly, we appear to be righteous. I did this when I tried to live the Sermon on the Mount out of my own power. You may have done it in attempting to keep the Ten Commandments. But if the deliverance is only "skin-deep," it is of no value. You can eliminate the cobweb, but if you don't catch the spider, he'll build another one!

Similarly, you can crush sin, but if you don't get at the root of it, it will break out again! Jesus referred to this type of deliverance, a form of hypocrisy, when He likened some people to whited sepulchres: white-washed on the outside but *full of dead men's bones!* (Matt. 23:27, italics added).

The difference between inward attitude and outward behavior, or complete and incomplete deliverance, is aptly illustrated by two stories. In the first, a father tells his son several times to sit down, but the little boy ignores his father's order. Finally, in anger, the father thunders, "Sit down!" This time the child obeys, but as he does, he mutters in a low voice, "I may be sitting down on the outside, but inside I'm still standing up!"

In the second story, a little boy calls out to his mother from upstairs after the bedtime ritual has ended, "Mom, bring me a drink of water, please."

His mother replies, "No! Go to sleep!"

"Mom!"

"Go to sleep!"

There is silence for a moment, then the little boy calls out again, "Mom!"

"GO - TO - SLEEP!"

This time there is a long silence. Then, "Mom!"

"Will you go to sleep? If I have to come upstairs to you, I will give you a good hiding!"

Mother's threat is followed by a long, long silence. At last the little fellow has gone to sleep, surely. But, no...a long while later, a pathetic voice cries out, "Mom, when you come upstairs to give me a good hiding, bring me a drink of water!"

Only a heart deliverance is a true deliverance. We

cannot eliminate failure by striving to change our outward behavior; our behavior is not the root of the problem.

Are Prayer and Fasting the Key?

Many declare that the key to freedom, success and power with God is prayer and fasting. To substantiate their claim, they quote the words of Jesus: "This kind cometh not out but by prayer and fasting" (see Mark 9:29). While I dare not say that they are wrong, I do say that they are not necessarily right!

The greater includes the lesser, so prayer and fasting may well be on the way to finding the key that will break the vicious circle so many are in or tear down the seemingly impenetrable wall they are running their heads up against. Their only consolation is like that of the man in the asylum who, when asked why he kept running his head at the wall, said, "It's so lovely when you stop doing it!"

Allow me to put this question to those who are fasting and praying: *Why* are you doing it? What is the *motive* that impels you to fast or pray?

What I do in God's sight is not so important as *why* I am doing it!

Doing the right thing with the wrong motive and without faith is like having a car with no gas. *It won't go!* Without faith, it is *impossible* to please God (see Heb. 11:6). Better to have a scooter with gas in the tank than a Rolls Royce revelation without faith!

Of what use is the Rolls Royce, untaxed, no license, rusting in the garage? But make no mistake about this: It is *much* better to have a Rolls Royce *and* gas! The right action and the right motive undergirded by faith will take you anywhere you want to go.

A man could fast and then write a book on it entitled *How I Fasted for Forty Days* with the motive of letting people see how wonderful he is. Such a man would do well to fast from living to people instead of fasting from food. Jesus said, "How can ye believe, which receive honour *one of another,* and *seek not* the honour that cometh *from God* only?" (John 5:44, italics added). Again, He said, "When you fast, wash your face and tell no man" (see Matt. 6:1-18, esp. v. 17; see also Is. 58). Fasting and praying that is undertaken to impress others is of no benefit.

Only prayer that is born of the Spirit and led of the Spirit is acceptable to God. James says, "Ye ask amiss, that ye may consume it upon your lusts" (James 4:3). As the Saviour slept, the disciples prayed, "Lord, save us: we perish," in the midst of the storm on the lake (Matt. 8:25). They were afraid for their lives!

If they had had real faith, they would not have prayed, they would have rested. As the hymn-writer says: "No waters can swallow the ship where lies, the Master of ocean and earth and skies!" This is not a criticism of the disciples; it is a statement of fact. Maybe if we had been there, we would have cried out for Jesus along with the loudest! The point is that the motive behind our prayers is what counts.

Are we willing to let God reveal our true motives?

Somewhere in the past I read a story of a young Irish policeman who found a dead horse in, I think it was MacConachie Street, and because he couldn't spell the name of the street in his notebook, he pulled the horse around the corner into King Street!

How many of us have pulled our dead horses around the corner because we would not have *truth?*

Well, do we want reality or not? Most of us have heard of the ostrich's supposed habit of sticking its head in the sand and thinking that, because it can't *see,* it can't *be seen.* I don't know whether this habit is actually common to ostriches, but I do know that it is to *man!*

Will you have truth in the inward parts? (See Ps. 51.)

Are you willing to be x-rayed by God's Holy Spirit? To be stripped to be clothed? To be emptied to be filled? "He taketh away the first, that He may establish the second" (Heb. 10:9). Maybe you will have to say, as I have had to, "Lord, I am not willing, but I am *willing* to be made willing. Work in me to will and to do of Your good pleasure" (see Phil. 2:13).

God declares: "Sin shall *not* have dominion over you"; "If God be for [you], who can be against [you]?"; and "In all these things [you] are *more than conquerors*" (Rom. 6:14; 8:31,37, italics added). We understand from His words that victory is the divine plan for *your* life! For *my* life! But how many Christians ever see the fulfillment of the plan of God for their lives?

"When [Jesus] was come near, he beheld the city, and wept over it, Saying, 'If thou hadst known, even thou, at least in this thy day, the things which belong unto thy peace! but now they are hid from thine eyes...because thou knewest not the time of thy visitation'" (Luke 19:42,44).

How many, in eternity, will look into the book of what *might have been* with bitter regret? It will be too late then! We are meant to be victorious, but without the master key, we are destined to fail. Since the value of prayer and fasting is determined by motive, they cannot be the key we are looking for.

Is Faith the Key?

At this point I would redirect your attention to faith. Faith is *a* key. Is it *the* key?

"Well," you say, "Jesus told us, 'Only believe'" (see Luke 8:50). Like prayer and fasting, faith may be well on the way to finding the key, and of necessity must be, because without it, we cannot please God; but is this finality?

If it is, we have now found the key! Go on, try it! Only

believe! And make no mistake about it, this *is* the Word
of God: *Only* believe!

Obstacles to Faith

But just when it appears that we have attained the
goal, we are faced with this realization: there are obsta-
cles to faith! One of them is the fleshly tendency to live to
people rather than to God. As mentioned earlier, Jesus
said, "How can ye believe, which receive honour one of
another?" (John 5:44). The principle that causes us to
live to man will hinder the growth of faith like a cankerworm will blight a plant! If I am living to man, I may be
in a position of wanting to believe and yet cannot.

This uncomfortable position puts us out with God, for
while God will not *accept* the works of the flesh, God
expects the works of faith. "Faith without works is dead"
(James 2:20). Your faith is in His Word; His Word is a
fact; and therefore you *act* on a *fact!* And *if you don't act,
you don't believe!*

The angel of the Lord did not call out to Abraham to
prevent him from killing Isaac *until* Abraham, in faith,
"stretched forth his hand, and took the knife to slay
his son" (Gen. 22:10-12). Now I understand! While
Abraham was *not* justified by a work of the flesh (that
is, by the act of raising his hand to kill Isaac), he *was*
justified by a work of faith (trusting God to fulfill the
promise of making him the father of many nations).
He "believed God, and it was counted unto him for
righteousness" (Rom. 4:3).

Another obstacle to faith is allowing our own experience to be the foundation for it. Most of us are familiar
with the type of situation in which a person is trusting
the Lord for healing. Maybe we have even done things
like the young man who took his spectacles off, jumped
on them in the name of Jesus and then three months
later secretly, and almost ashamedly, sidled into the
optician's for a new pair!

Again, how many of us, with great gusto and loud hallelujahs, have thrown our pipes, tobaccos and cigarettes into the fire and then gone back to the soothing weed afterwards!

Why?

Well, answer it, *why?* Are you prepared to water down the standard and make God a liar because of *your* experience? Does believing come by feeling, seeing, or having, or does it come by hearing?

Still another obstacle to faith is a lack of love. Faith works by love. You will find it very difficult to believe God after an argument with your wife! How can you love and believe God whom you don't see, if you can't love your brother whom you do see? (See 1 John 4:20.)

This is your trouble: You do not see God in the situation that makes you fall out with God via your wife. You see only your wife! Joseph said to his brothers who sold him into Egypt, "It was not you that sent me here; it was God" (see Gen. 45:8).

Remember these words, "When were you sick, Lord, and we visited you not?" Jesus answered, " 'Verily I say unto you, Inasmuch as ye did it not to one of the least of these, ye did it not to *me*' " (Matt. 25:44-45, italics added). So faith can be hindered or made ineffective by a hidden principle that operates in man and that makes him fall out with God and his brother. We shall see later what this principle is.

The Greater Includes the Lesser

Many keys, but only one master key. How easy to believe that because I have *some* keys, I have *the* key!

Psychology, for example, is a key, but not the key. The Bible (the greatest book on psychology) does not so much stress the *educating* of the mind as it does the *renewing* of the mind. "Be ye transformed [that is, changed] by the *renewing* of your mind" (Rom. 12:2, italics added). "Let this mind be in you, which was also in Christ Jesus" (Phil. 2:5).

"Good" is the enemy of "best"; a key will unlock a door, but *the key* will unlock every door! The greater includes the lesser, but the lesser does *not* include the greater. Though we have discovered many keys, we are still not in possession of the master.

FIVE

THINE IS THE GLORY

While most Christians readily agree that the highest in God is His glory (how often have we heard the prayer "And we shall be careful to give Thee all the glory"), many refuse to concede that the lowest in man is *not* sin!

We are now coming to the master key, the key for avoiding sin and for turning failure into success. At this point I very earnestly say to you, Watch the witness!

Jesus said of the Holy Spirit: "He will guide you into *all* truth" (John 16:13, italics added). Because the Holy Spirit is holy, He never witnesses to a lie. "It is the

Spirit that beareth witness, because the Spirit is truth" (1 John 5:6).

But this witness is not outside us. "He that believeth on the Son of God *hath the witness in himself*" (1 John 5:10, italics added). Every man needs a personal revelation of truth, and a mental grasp in his head is no substitute for it. There is a difference between a worldly man who knows all *about* Jesus and a Christian (born again of the Spirit) who *knows* Jesus!

Before you read on, take time to acknowledge your utter helplessness and confess your absolute need of the Spirit of God to give you light, life and revelation. Don't fall into the trap of thinking that you know what the glory of God is; a rational understanding is no substitute for the revelation of the Spirit.

Sin Is a Consequence, Not a Cause

If you admit that the glory of God is the highest in God, are you prepared to make room for this: that sin is *not* the lowest in man? In other words, as I have said before, sin is a result; it is not a cause, but a consequence.

Let me show you what I mean. If sin is number one in man, then righteousness is number one in God; if unbelief is number one in man, then faith is number one in God; but if neither of these is number one, then we have an entirely different order. In reality, the glory of God, or credit due to Him, is number one. The faith of God is number two, and the righteousness of God is number three. Similarly, the glory of man, which is his pride, is number one; the unbelief of man is number two; and the sin of man is number three.

The book of Genesis bears this order out. When Satan first tempted Eve to eat of the tree of the knowledge of good and evil, he appealed to her pride, "In the day ye eat thereof, then your eyes shall be opened, and *ye shall be as gods*" (Gen. 3:5, italics added).

Look at the process Eve went through in taking the fruit. The Bible says she saw that the tree was "good for food" and "to be desired to make one wise" (Gen. 3:6). So her pride caused her to reject God's Word ("In the day that thou eatest thereof thou shalt surely die") in unbelief and fall into sin (Gen. 2:17; 3:6). Face this in your own life: you were never in sin without first being in unbelief; and you arrived in unbelief because of the pride or self-glory of your heart, which caused you to become your own god and reject God as God.

Sin always comes out of unbelief. Unbelief is always the expression of pride or self-glory. One, two, three! Pride (number one) begets unbelief (number two) which produces sin (number three). Thus pride, not sin, is the cause of failure. Pride is the spider!

Notice that God has grace for sin, but not for unbelief or pride. Unbelief in the Israelites prevented them from entering the Promised Land: "They could not enter in because of their unbelief" (Heb. 3:19). Unbelief in the people of His own country prevented Jesus from performing many miracles among them: "He did not many mighty works there because of their unbelief" (Matt. 13:58).

It is vital to know what God *will* do and what He *won't* do. He will forgive the man who is wrong but not the man with a whitewash brush called pride who pretends he isn't wrong! He will *not* forgive pride. Rather, the Scriptures tell us that "God resisteth the proud" (1 Pet. 5:5). So don't pray about pride or ask God to forgive you; humble yourself under His mighty hand (1 Pet. 5:6). This is the only appropriate remedy for attempting to take God's glory for yourself.

The Scriptures make it very clear to whom all glory belongs. Isaiah 42:8 says, "I am the Lord: that is my name: and my glory will I *not* give to another" (italics added). Isaiah 48:11 repeats God's words, "I will not give my glory unto another." Jesus taught His disciples to pray to the Father, "*Thine* is the kingdom, and the power, *and the glory,* for ever, Amen" (Matt. 6:13, italics added). And Romans 11:36 claims of the Lord, "For *of* him, and *through* him, and *to* him, are *all things*: to whom be glory for ever. Amen" (italics added).

By glory we mean credit due. God cannot share the glory because *all* things are *of Him and Him alone.* He would virtually deny Himself. This He cannot do (2 Tim. 2:13). If only half the work is God's, then half the credit is God's; but if all the work is God's, then all the glory is God's!

The Scriptures do not put God's possession of the glory in future tense. Thine *is* the glory, not Thine *will be* the glory! The glory never leaves His hand. While man seeks to rob God of His glory, there is a divine thermostatic control that operates as soon as man attempts to touch it!

Just as a thermostat automatically controls the flow of cool air in a home, so God, the God of circumstances—of whom are all things—has everything under His control.

His glory *never* leaves His hand!

God Resists the Proud

There are examples in Scripture of men who exalted themselves. Nebuchadnezzar was one of these. As he walked in the palace of the kingdom of Babylon, he said, "Is not this great Babylon, that I have built...by the might of *my* power?" (Dan. 4:29-30, italics added). He tried to take the glory for what God had done.

Nebuchadnezzar's punishment was swift and severe. The "great" king was reduced to the state of an animal bereft of reason. He dwelt with the beasts of the field; his body was wet with the dew of heaven; he ate grass with the oxen; and his hair became like eagles' feathers and his nails like birds' claws. He was a lunatic without an asylum, stripped on one principle: "Every one that exalteth himself shall be abased" (Luke 18:14).

Nebuchadnezzar started out giving God the glory. Addressing "all people, nations and languages that dwell in all the earth," he said, "'I thought it good to shew the signs and wonders that the high God hath wrought toward me. How great are his signs! and how mighty are his wonders!'" (Dan. 4:1-3). He was like King Uzziah who, when he first began to reign, "did that which was right in the sight of the Lord" and "sought God" (2 Chron. 26:4-5).

Both kings prospered as long as they magnified the Lord. Of Uzziah, Scripture says, "His name spread far abroad; for he was marvellously helped" (v. 15). But when they became proud, both of them were brought down. Uzziah was marvellously helped, "*till* he was strong." When he became strong, "his heart was lifted up *to his destruction*" (v. 16, italics added).

In Acts 12 we read of another prideful man: Herod. Verse 2 tells us that Herod "stretched forth his hands to vex certain of the church. And he killed James the brother of John." Later he sat upon his throne in royal apparel and delivered an oration before the people of Tyre and Sidon (v. 21). When they heard him, they said, "It is the voice of a god, and not of a man" (v. 22). As soon as they made this declaration—the Scriptures say *immediately*—"the angel of the Lord smote [Herod]...and he was eaten of worms" (v. 23).

Why did God smite him? Because he slew James? No. Because the people tried to exalt him? No. Because "*he gave not God the glory*" (Acts 12:23, italics added).

These three examples of God's response to the proud are not exceptions, for "every one that is proud in heart is an abomination to the Lord" and none "shall...be unpunished" (Prov. 16:5).

Sin is not the cause of sin; pride is! The Church has

never effectively dealt with the sin problem because it has never gotten down to the root, the cause: pride. For the consequence—sin—there is grace, pardon, the blood of Jesus. For the cause—pride—the burden is on the individual: "Humble [yourself]" (1 Pet. 5:6).

All God does with the proud is resist them and abase them (1 Pet. 5:5; Dan. 4:37). As long as men point the finger at sin, whatever it may be—lust, drug addiction, hatred, drunkenness, violent abuse and so on—they are dealing with only the effect and not the cause.

God's Order

To illustrate: Say that I have one silver dollar, two silver quarters and three silver dimes.

Now the *numerical* value of three dimes (from the standpoint of quantity) is greater than the numerical value of one dollar—three is greater than one—but the *sterling* value of the one is greater than the sterling value of the three. I would rather have one silver dollar than three silver dimes!

In the same way, God has an order that is vital for me to recognize. Just as one dollar, one quarter and one dime are not the same, pride, unbelief and sin are not the same. There is a different assessment of grading. There is a one, two, three with God and a one, two, three with man.

Neither are glory, faith and righteousness the same. The worst in man is not his sin; the highest in man is not his righteousness. "'Except your righteousness exceed the righteousness of the scribes and Pharisees,'" said Jesus, "'ye shall in no case enter into the kingdom of heaven'" (Matt. 5:20).

Remember the story of the righteous Pharisee strutting in the presence of God as he boasted of his fasting and tithing? His righteousness was the filthy rags of *self*-righteousness; it was not "of faith," and it was not to the glory of God, so he was not justified before God (see Luke 18:10-14).

On the other hand, the publican, who recognized that he had no righteousness within himself, was justified. "'God be merciful to me a sinner,'" he said (Luke 18:13). Why was he justified? Because he humbled himself.

Beneath man's sin is unbelief. No man ever sinned who was not first in unbelief; no man ever arrived in unbelief but that he first exalted himself in pride and thus chose his own glory instead of God's. He chose to *be* a god instead of *having* a God!

Self-righteousness is a spurious coin that is not accepted at the counter of heaven's bank because it did not come from the Royal Mint. Anything that puts honor on flesh *must* be *wrong*, while anything that puts honor on God *must* basically be *right!*

What is the government's attitude toward a man who says, "Me? Oh, yes, I am a rich man! Dollars? I've thousands of them! I make my own! Here, catch, have a bundle!" This man is a danger to the structure of our society. He is a forger, his money is counterfeit, and he must be put in prison.

"He that climbeth up *some other way*, the same is a thief and a robber" (John 10:1, italics added). If you are not living to the glory of God, if you are seeking your own glory, you are robbing God of His glory. You are a thief and a robber!

Every bank note must have the official water mark on it and the name of the cashier appointed. Every child of God must believe on the name of His Son (1 John 5:13). There is no other name, no other way! "This is he that came by water and blood, even Jesus Christ" (1 John 5:6).

I used to feel sorry for the man in the New Testament who was turned out of the marriage feast because he didn't have a wedding garment on. I thought, *Poor man, perhaps he could not afford to buy one! It seems a bit harsh for him to be cast "into outer darkness"* (see Matt. 22:10-13).

Then someone pointed out to me that in the East, the wedding garment is provided by the host. There is no greater insult to him than not to accept his provision. The guests had to come the right way in order to stay at the feast. Similarly, we must come the right way in order to be received by God.

The Function of the Heart

The Word of God declares, "With the heart man believeth" (Rom. 10:10). So then, the function of man's heart is to believe. This unseen function of the heart, when properly exercised, allows us to bow to God. When not exercised, it causes us, in pride and defiance, to lift up against God.

The spiritual function of the heart operates continually in every man, just like the physical function of pumping blood. But while the physical beat of the human heart is regular, each time expelling the same amount of blood, the spiritual "beat" can alternate between belief and unbelief. Think of the *spiritual* effects over the course of a lifetime! Every moment of every day I am either bowing or rising: bowing and glorifying God or rising and glorifying myself. No wonder Jesus said, "Blessed are the pure in heart: for they shall see God" (Matt. 5:8).

So, then, finality is *glory,* either man's or God's. Which shall it be? The Lord Jesus declared, "*Thine* is the glory," to His Father (see Matt. 6:13). Will we follow suit?

I cannot see a sunset, a foggy morning, a roast beef dinner, a sink full of dirty dishes or a pretty girl without having some sort of response within. In the same way, I cannot experience the ups and downs of everyday life without choosing whether or not to see the hand of God in each situation. My response will determine my reaction.

If I see God in His creation, provision and grace, I will glorify Him and give Him thanks. If I see Him in a challenging circumstance, I will bow to the infinite wisdom that permits what the almighty power could prevent.

I may face a situation that I would never choose if I ordered my own life. If I see God in it, I bow; if I don't, I rise. The decision to bow or rise is being made every day, nay, every moment of every day, by every man. It is being made every moment by *you.*

"The four and twenty elders and the four beasts fell down and worshipped God...saying, Amen; Alleluia" (Rev. 19:4). Bowing was their continual response to the presence of God.

If I meet and see God in my circumstances, then two words suffice as my reaction to them: *Amen* and *alleluia.* This is where Jesus lives. He said, "I and My Father are one" (John 10:30). Strangely enough, the fall of man (sin) is actually the rise, the place where I rise up and refuse to bow. My rising up breaks communion.

God Lets Us Know Whether We Are "In" or "Out"

Now then, upon every judgment that I pronounce, upon every function of my heart wherein I either bow or rise, God puts His seal or witness of either pleasure or displeasure.

Paul told the Colossians, "Let the peace of God rule in your hearts" for good reason (Col. 3:15). There is purpose in the peace. It is not just a nice feeling to be enjoyed as a direct indication of the mind of God on my judgments; it is an umpire or referee that tells me when I am "safe," a thermometer that operates inside me for the glory of God.

By pain or pleasure, God expresses in me an independent witness that tells me when I am "out" and when I am "in," when I am bowing and when I am rising.

Monotony, boredom, frustration, irritation, fear, depression, gloom, anger, envy, worry, hatred and other negative emotions are all feelings that are occasioned by my rising up against God. They are a sign of God's disapproval of the judgments my heart has "passed" on His dealings with me.

God resists the proud, and *everyone* that exalts himself shall be abased! (See 1 Pet. 5:5 and Luke 18:14.) My bad feelings express the resistance of God toward me.

In the same way, when I bow to God, the peace and joy in my heart express His pleasure. They tell me when I am "in" with Him. So every moment of my life, I can know whether I am "in" or "out" with God. The Scriptures confirm this claim: "Thou wilt keep him in perfect peace, whose mind is stayed on thee" (Is. 26:3).

The following song is an appropriate commentary on the benefits of continually bowing, of continually saying "Amen" to God.

What is that which harms thee if thou sayest amen,
Every grave a cradle of fresh bliss again,
Let not understanding look upon each grave,
Faith has better eyesight than all Nature gave.
Amen has within it, powers yet unknown,
Unfound faith is hiding long before it's grown,
Amen has much sweetness while things are still
    sour,
Amen is the father of the gladsome hour.
Who withholds his Amen finds the source of pain,
'Tis a river flowing, pain and pain again,
Amen once repeated finds itself in glee,
Flowing, flowing, flowing through eternity.
Amen is the finger opening to our sight,
Anthems loud and glorious made for darkest night,
Amen touches heartstrings, long at rest in sleep,
Making chords so wondrous rise from every deep.
           —*Harold Webster, unpublished*

Peace and joy accompany bowing. God doesn't want a lot of salt zombies like Lot's wife who are looking back to what they have left, moaning for the leeks and onions of Egypt instead of enjoying the milk and honey of Canaan (see Gen. 19:26). "The *joy* of the Lord is your strength" (Neh. 8:10, italics added). "Amen" to God isn't a dirge; there is music in it!

SIX

PRIDE: THE GLORY OF MAN

In the previous chapter we established the fact that *God's glory never leaves His hand.* His alone is the glory; thus, man cannot actually rob God of the credit that is due Him. However, he seeks to do so and is therefore guilty of stealing the glory. He is answerable for that which he attempts to do.

Man's attempt to steal God's glory occurs when his heart functions out of order and instead of bowing, rises in self-exaltation (pride). More damnable than any sin, more vile than any injury a man can inflict on his brother, is this refusal to bow to God, this rebellion of the heart in its uprising as it seeks to unseat God from His throne—to become a god instead of having a God!

It is the same response Eve had when Satan tempted her to eat the forbidden fruit, insisting that she and Adam would "be as gods" (Gen. 3:5).

The Nature of Pride

Pride is the treason of the creature against his Creator. When a man sees his self-glory or pride for what it is instead of seeing it as "pardonable pride," then he sees it as God sees it. When he tries to excuse it, he is like the Pharisees of whom Jesus said, "Ye are they which justify yourselves before men; but God knoweth your hearts: for that which is highly esteemed among men *is abomination in the sight of God*" (Luke 16:15, italics added). "My thoughts are not your thoughts," says the Lord (Is. 55:8).

Pride is always a lie. It is the very disposition of the devil, the father of all lies, who "abode not in the truth" (John 8:44).

As we receive revelation about the true nature of pride, we see it for what it is: a many-headed monster that attempts to wrest God from His throne and that is the contender of the right of God to rule His own universe.

Many seemingly innocent activities have pride as a motivating factor. A continual glancing in the mirror, for example, cannot be dismissed as just the whim of a young girl to look her best or the fleeting vanity of youth expressed in the tilt of a hat or the style of the hair, but must be acknowledged as a challenger of the very throne of God.

Compared to the proverbial cat, which has nine lives, pride has nine hundred lives: pride of race, pride of face, pride of place and even pride of grace. I need grace for grace (John 1:16). Pride is so subtle that one can become aware of its hideousness and humble on an issue and then finish up by being proud of one's humility! Hardly has the head of this Goliath rolled in the dust ere it is growing again at the point of the very sword that beheaded it.

Of all the many angles and faces of pride, or man's glory, spiritual pride is probably the worst, and what makes it so bad for the victims of the "disease" is that pride is oblivious; those in the most advanced stages are the least aware of their condition. Often they don't even recognize that they're ill!

The Remedy for Pride

What is God's response to those who are afflicted? The Bible says that God *resists* the proud and that *everyone* who is proud in heart is an abomination to the Lord (see 1 Pet. 5:5; Prov. 16:5). Thus it is imperative that the disease be diagnosed.

Once it is, what is the remedy? The remedy for sin (the consequence of pride) is the blood of Jesus Christ. The remedy for pride? Humbling oneself! First Peter 5:6 directs us to "Humble [our]selves therefore under the mighty hand of God." If the blood of Christ were effective for man's pride, then all men would be saved, but the word of God declares, "Behold the Lamb of God, which taketh away the *sin* [not the pride] of the world" (John 1:29, italics added).

Physical life began when God breathed into the nostrils of Adam the breath of life. Life continues as long as man keeps breathing. See how long you can live while holding your breath! In the same way, the Spirit of God breathed, and we were quickened spiritually, but our spiritual lives, for their development and maintenance, demand communion. Communion requires faith, and faith requires us to bow. The Scriptures tell us that "the just shall live by faith," but because of the fall, man must bow to receive it (Rom. 1:7). Constant bowing is as vital, as necessary, as constant breathing!

The Lord Jesus Christ was sinless, yet *He* humbled Himself (see Phil. 2:8). How much more should *you and I* do so! Did He not say, as I have mentioned before, "How can ye believe, which receive honour one of another, and *seek not* the honour that cometh from *God only?*" (John 5:44, italics added).

Indeed, "How *can* ye believe?" A question without an answer! If you live to man instead of to God, your faith will diminish, communion will wane and you will become spiritually asthmatical, having difficulty "breathing."

What makes men respond differently to the situations they face? Some receive truth; some do not. Some refuse to bow. Why? Man refuses to humble himself under the mighty hand of God because of his pride, which is his glory.

The remedy for pride is not cleansing, but humbling! I cannot use the excuse that I am unable to humble, because my heart was *made* to bow even as my lungs were made to breathe. *Will* not bow, yes; but *cannot*, never!

It is as alien to the divine plan for man not to bow in his heart as it is for him not to breathe with his lungs. Man was made to breathe, and he was also made to bow.

God's Plan

Of course, I could hold my breath and die. But if I intend to go on living, I must breathe. Will yesterday's breathing suffice for today's living? Will yesterday's bowing release me from today's responsibility to humble? While an iron lung or artificial respiration may substitute for my breathing in an emergency, ultimately mechanized or "pinch-hit" breathing is not God's plan. Similarly, while God may abase the creature from without through circumstances, humiliation is no substitute for my humbling and bowing in my heart.

The pressure of circumstances, like the stake that the young sapling is bound to, show me the way I must grow; the compulsory mile precedes the voluntary mile that I take once I humble myself. God will use the whole range, if necessary, from stomach ulcers and leaky taps to an untidy husband and a nagging mother-in-law, to show me His will and hold me down where I ought to be, "lest I should be exalted *above measure*" (2 Cor. 12:7, italics added). But ultimately abasement via circumstances is not His plan.

In the day of measure, man has been permitted a measure of exaltation. As soon as he has reached this point, which is as invisible, but nevertheless as real as the line of the equator, then an inexorable principle takes over. What is it? The principle of the glory of God!

God's glory is, as it were, thermostatically controlled; once the predetermined limit of human exaltation is reached, the principle clicks into operation and God says, "My glory will I *not* give to another!" (Is. 42:8, italics added).

In the day of fullness, man will no longer be permitted even a measure of exaltation. God's ultimate plan is for us to continually humble ourselves and give Him *all* the glory!

Oh, dear reader, if anything needs to be indelibly written on your heart and mine it is this: God *will not* give His glory to another! He never, never permits it to leave His hand. You may think, like the student driver, that because you have the steering wheel in your hand you are in control, but what you do not realize is that God's car has dual controls; *He can put the brake on at any time!*

He who upholds all things by the word of His power can wrestle with Jacob and touch the hollow of his thigh till the sinew shrinks, cause a storm and a great fish to deal with the runaway Jonah, and make a donkey speak to Balaam (see Heb. 1:3; Gen. 32:24-25,32; Jon. 1:4-17; Num. 22:28-39). He commands every caterpillar, cankerworm and locust, and, with one imperious claim, calls them "my great army"—the great army He once sent among the Israelites (Joel 2:25).

Who made all the brains, hearts, lungs, eyes, ears, kidneys and so on in the universe? Who holds *you* up? *Of Him* are all things! What an insignificant word "of" is! Consider it! Put this book down for two minutes and consider the import of the statement, *Of Him* are *all things* (see Rom. 11:36). God has only to lift His little finger, as it were, to put the brake on and bring you into line! He can touch your heart, your nerves or your limbs at any moment and use the devil to do it; He can send the messenger of Satan to buffet you. Why? Lest you should be exalted above measure!

You have blamed this one, that one or the devil for your troubles, and all the time it has been Father! Why? Why has your heavenly Father, who loves you, permitted in His wisdom what He could have kept from you in His power? Reflect on this question from the point of view of a natural father. Why would he shape and mold his child's life? Why not, rather, let the child have his own way—spit on the floor—throw gravy in his mother's face—make a bonfire in the middle of the bedroom floor if he wants to?

Why not? Because the social misfits, the hooligans, the murderers of today were the sweet little horrors of yesterday who were left to have their own way. No greater punishment can any man have than to be left to have his own way!

"*Thy will* be done in earth"—in *me*—"as it is in heaven" (Matt. 6:10, italics added). As I humble to the truth and yield my will, two essential points become clear.

First, I can humble myself only *under the mighty*

hand; that is, only according to God's direction. God will show me the place. There is an appropriate counter at which to buy the truth for each situation. You don't purchase vegetables at a newsstand or burgers and fries at a clothing store! I have to humble myself to receive truth at the counter *indicated by the mighty hand.* Confiding to the pastor about an adulterous affair, for example, is no substitute for confessing to the wife.

Second, I do not humble to man! I humble *before* man but *to God!*

To summarize: Humbling is a way of life; nay, it is *the* way of life. If the sinless Son of God humbled Himself, so must we! God commands us, through His servant Paul, to "Let this mind be in you, which was also in Christ Jesus." What mind? The mind of a man "who, being in the form of God, thought it not robbery to be equal with God: But made himself *of no reputation,* and took upon him the form of a servant, and was made in the likeness of men: And being found in fashion as a man, *he humbled himself,* and *became obedient* unto death" (Phil. 2:5-8, italics added).

Jesus made Himself *of no reputation.* He *humbled Himself.* We must follow His example. How?

Humble Yourself

My advice is simple: Rather than exalting yourself, humble yourself! In the past, you took the highest seat; now take the lowest. You talked about *you*—what you had done and where you had been—"I, I, I". Now talk about *Him.* Challenge yourself! In all that you do and say, ask: "Why am I doing this? Why am I saying that?" Remember: *What* you do doesn't count with God, but *why* you do it does!

If your motive in all that you do and say is to give glory to God, both your habit (your attire) and your habits (your customary ways of doing things) will change: You will dress differently, talk differently and

54

love differently! You will stop seeing yourself as the hero or heroine in every Bible story.

If you are always Mary, having chosen the better part to sit at Jesus' feet while your sister is busy serving the food and washing the dishes, consider this: Though Jesus implied that Martha ought to have ceased working and joined Mary in listening to His word, there are a lot of Marys who would do well to imitate the Master on another occasion and "take a towel" (see Luke 10:38-42; John 13:4-5).

Revelation can come just as easily at the kitchen sink as at a Bible school—perhaps more easily, for He *gives grace* to the *humble* and *hides things* from the *wise and prudent* (see 1 Pet. 5:5; Matt. 11:25).

Humility is a hard word. No wonder they crucified the Truth! I can lustily sing, "Where He may lead, I will follow" and then complain about having to take out the garbage!

We need to take a closer look at ourselves. The Scottish poet Robert Burns once said: "Oh, wad to God the gift wad gie us, Tae see ourselves as ithers see us!"

This comment, I believe, was occasioned by the sight of a large and lofty lady who was majestically proceeding down the church aisle like a liner coming up river and who, unbeknownst to herself, had a spider going up and down like a yo yo from the back of her hat as it spun its web. Oh, would to God the gift would give us, to see ourselves as *He* sees us! *Or could we bear it?* Could we handle the truth?

You Bow to What You Believe

What a man believes rules him! He does not rule what he believes. This is important! When I believe, I bow.

What am I bowing to? Superstition? Fashion? Tradition? Custom? Other men? Lies? Or truth? Never before was the man in the street subject to such an

onslaught of canvassing, plotting and scheming intended to woo him as now. From newspaper column and
shop window, from T.V. screen and billboard, the
avalanche descends. The unsuspecting public slowly
but inscrutably are being shaped to believe what the
commercial juggernaut decrees.

Our children repeat advertising jargon like they once
repeated nursery rhymes! Their parents believe that the
joy of living is in a can of beans. Someone has said that
a mere handful of masterminds are able to influence
millions of women through the articles of women's mag-
azines, by informing them what their vital statistics
should be, what they should and should not eat, what
they should wear, and what length they should keep
their skirts and hair.

In other words, we believe, and therefore, we bow. *It
matters what people think of me! I must keep up with the
Jones's!* "All we like sheep," says Isaiah 53:6, "have
gone astray." Hypnotized by public opinion, we, like the
soldier in the following story, believe what everybody
else believes.

The dying soldier on the battlefield was asked by the
padre what he believed.

"I believe what the church believes," he gasped.

"Which church? What does your church believe?"

"The church believes what I believe!"

"Well, what do you both believe?"

"We both believe alike," was the reply!

When we believe what men put forth rather than what
God says, we bow to the wrong "authority."

Bowing to God from the heart must be like breathing
with the lungs—continual. To every issue in life you
will have a reaction: let it be the right one! Just as the
cash register in the grocery store rings up the amount
of a purchase, the piano responds to a note pressed
and the video camera captures what the eye and ear for
a fleeting moment have witnessed, so your heart and

mine are registering, registering *all the time!*

What is finally on my slate? That depends on me. "As [a man] thinketh in his heart, so is he" (Prov. 23:7). As long as I am in the probationary school of life, a past judgment can be erased by a present one. I am able to own up to what I am, in order to disown what I am. By an act of humbling to the truth, I can say, "This is me, but *I am sorry!*" And it is here that grace and truth, the subjects of the next chapter, come in.

SEVEN

IF YOU WANT
MORE GRACE, EMBRACE
MORE TRUTH

Grace [the undeserved favor of God] and truth [reality] came by Jesus Christ" (John 1:17). God has married them, and that which God has joined together, man cannot separate—there is no divorce here. All men seek after, and desire more of, the grace of God. They may not want the God of grace, but they cannot live without the grace of God!

The young man in the process of courting woos his sweetheart with pound boxes of chocolates—boating trips up the river on a Saturday afternoon—soft lights and music in some cozy little cafe. He will spend and

spend on her, lavish a thousand attentions on her!
Why? In order to draw her to himself!
What is his reaction if she takes all his gifts and goes
off with another? Ex. 20:5 tells us God's response to
similar behavior on our part: "I the Lord thy God am a
jealous God." God is the only One in finality who has a
right to be jealous.
There is no sin in God's jealousy, no unrighteousness. The glory, or credit due Him, is His by right of creation and redemption. Of Him are all things! We have no
rights. We cannot even curse Him except with the lungs
and the air He gave us!
If you, like Jonah, run away from Him, there is no
sea you can cross, no mountain you can climb, no
cave you can hide in, that doesn't belong to Him!
"The earth is the *Lord's* and the fulness thereof" (Ps.
24:1, italics added). Trespassers will be prosecuted!
Can you fly to some far-flung outpost of the universe? He owns all the galaxies—all the Milky Ways.
Falling worlds, darting hither and thither in their
appointed orbits like the teeming fish of the oceans,
were all created by Him.
The mind reels as it attempts to grasp what one light
year is; how much more when we consider that the light
from distant worlds, traveling at 186,000 miles per second, left its source before Jesus was born nearly 2,000
years ago! How great is our God!
Contemplate the graciousness and favor of God, who
upholds every function of your house of clay: Could you
make your own eye to see, ear to hear, heart to beat,
lungs to breathe, or brain to function? "In Him we live,
and move, and have our being" (Acts 17:28).
For every *recognized* function of your body there are
dozens and dozens of unperceived faculties you would
appreciate only if they ceased to operate. Only if a man
were reduced to a driveling, slavering, gibbering imbe-
cile staggering into blind oblivion would it be apparent

how utterly dependent the creature is upon the Creator. Have you ever thanked God for your reason?

We need the grace of God even to recognize the grace of God—"grace for grace" (John 1:16).

Whether we admit it or not, all of us seek the grace of God in our lives—health, wealth, prosperity, joy, peace, happiness—the things we wish each other every Christmastide on the cards we send. We need to recognize that God has a monopoly on them; He has no rival, no competitor. He is the sole distributor!

I need God's grace, but I cannot separate it from the truth. Grace is not provided merely to meet man's need. So, when I seek to lead Grace away from her betrothed spouse, she says, "Oh, no, I will not come unless you invite my husband, Mr. Truth, as well; we will come to your house together!"

This puts me on the spot! Do I want grace so that I may consume it upon my lusts, or do I want it to lead me to the truth, the glory of God?

The Grace of God Is for the Glory of God

The truth is that the grace of God is *first* for the glory of God and only incidentally to meet my need. God does not deliver me from my failure simply for the sake of delivering me. He delivers me for His glory, and if He is not getting the credit, He won't do the work! "I will *not* give my glory unto another" (Is. 48:11, italics added).

Many people are tied to pardoning grace who are longing for changing grace. The difference? "Oh, God, I'm sorry; I've done it again!" instead of "Praise God! The desire is gone!" Until I give God the glory due His name for pardoning grace, I am not likely to find changing grace. Both are for His glory, and if I have not rendered to Him for what I am already receiving, what evidence is there that I will for that which, as yet, I have not received? I am cheating on God! The credit is God's because the work is God's, and God will do the work when He gets the credit. If He is not getting the credit, He won't do the work: the evidence of my failure!

When I fail to give God the credit due Him, exalting myself in pride and thereby breaking the principle of the glory of God, He withdraws His grace. Without His grace, I experience failure. This is inevitable. Failure is nothing more than a withdrawal of the grace of God on a certain given point in my life.

To x-ray my failure, to break it up, to dissolve it, I must go back three, two, one. My failure (number three) occurs because I lack God's grace. I lack God's grace because I am in unbelief (number two). I am in unbelief because in my pride, instead of bowing to God, I set myself up in His place, turn a deaf ear to His voice and reject His Word (number one). On the basis that I am in pride, God resists me, and He does this by withdrawing His grace!

Let's look at a real-life example. Suppose a man steals a loaf of bread from the local bakery in order to feed his starving family. His stealing the bread is his sin (number three); the motivation for stealing it is his unbelief (number two). He rejects the promise of Philippians 4:19, "My God shall supply all [my] need," and sets himself up as God in seeking to meet the needs of his family himself by inappropriate means (number one).

Or suppose a woman gossips about her neighbor. Her gossiping is her sin, but she would never have arrived at it had she not, in her pride, set herself up as God and made a judgment about her neighbor's behavior. She goes past the Scriptural admonitions to avoid judging and to walk in love, doubting God's Word that He "will render to every man according to his deeds" (Rom. 2:6).

By these examples (and there are as many others as there are sins), we see that this is how it works: In my pride, I set myself up as God and make a judgment. God opposes me by removing His grace, for He "giveth grace [only] to the humble" (1 Pet. 5:5). The judgment leads to unbelief, and the unbelief leads to sin. The greater includes the lesser!

My sin or my failure (number three) is the inevitable consequence of my judgments (number one). This needs to be written in letters of fire in every life! "Judge not that ye be not judged" (Matt. 7:1). "Thou that judgest doest the same things" (Rom. 2:1). I dig my own grave when I judge.

Deliverance in Failure

There are two forms of deliverance relative to failure: deliverance *from* and deliverance *in.* Deliverance *from* is measure; deliverance *in* is fullness! The three Hebrews were delivered *in* Nebuchadnezzar's fiery furnace, not *from* it. God did not allow the fire to touch them. Daniel was delivered *in* the lions' den, not *from* it. God shut the lions' mouths.

You may suck peppermints in an effort to stop smoking; that's measure. Or God can just take the desire away; that's fullness. Pardoning grace versus changing grace!

Fullness in deliverance is primarily to glorify God and only incidentally to meet my need. My need can never be fully met in measure, and only when I seek the glory of God will my need be fully met. Many of us will never reach fullness in deliverance because we have never had fullness of truth, which is the glory of God.

As long as *you* want to be number one, seeking first to fill your own need rather than giving God glory, God will put you out; and when you say "Amen" to being left out, He will bring you in; so the sooner you are out, the sooner you will be in!

How important we are in our own eyes! Man and his need are only incidental. The gigantic truth of the universe is that *all* things are *of, through and to* the glory of God (see Rom. 11:36).

As you receive this truth, you will find that grace will automatically flow! In other words, the grace of God is divinely, thermostatically controlled, not in line with *your need*, but in line with *His glory!*

God's strength is made perfect in our weakness (2 Cor. 12:9). Jesus, the perfect man, was a helpless man. He declared, "I can *of mine own self* do nothing" (John 5:30, italics added). His grace, like a glove, is made to fit the hand of man's weakness, that the excellency of the power we wield may be of God and not of us and thus give glory to Him alone!

More Grace Requires More Truth

The point of all this is to say that the measure of the grace you are enjoying in your life is the measure of the truth you have received. If you require more grace, you need to receive more truth. To do this, you will have to humble yourself at the appropriate counter. Proverbs 23:23 says, "Buy the truth, and sell it not."

Many of us do not want to admit that we need more truth. We are like King Saul when he told the prophet Samuel, "I have performed the commandment of the Lord [relative to the utter destruction of the Amalekites]" (1 Sam. 15:13). God had told Saul to "go and smite Amalek, and *utterly destroy* all that they have," but Saul spared Agag, the king of the Amalekites, as well as the best of the livestock and "all that was good" (vv. 3,9, italics added). Yet Saul insisted that he had obeyed the voice of the Lord (v. 20).

Samuel caught Saul in his half truth; he asked him, "What meaneth then this bleating of the sheep in mine ears?" (v. 14). In other words, *Dead sheep don't bleat!*

All a child's begging for the ignition key of Daddy's car

will avail nothing. The child must live with Daddy, obey Daddy and be one with Daddy's mind and then, one day, to fulfill Father's will, he will be driving Father's car, which is not a toy or a plaything, but a vehicle for the greater expression of the Father's mind and plan and purpose. The journey from Daddy to Father is something in the child rather than in the Father.

How long does this journey take? Just as long as it takes the child to be able and willing to become *one* with the Father. He must grow in grace! Jesus says, "I have yet many things to say unto you, but ye cannot bear them now" (John 16:12).

One scripture many cannot bear calls us to present our bodies as a holy sacrifice to God. "I beseech you therefore, brethren, by the mercies of God, that ye present your bodies a living sacrifice, holy, acceptable unto God" (Rom. 12:1). Paul tells us that this is our "reasonable service" for the glory of God. "Your body is the temple of the Holy Ghost...and *ye are not your own*" (1 Cor. 6:19, italics added).

Yet tens of thousands of people have so abused their bodies with their unbridled appetites that they cannot even enjoy the doubtful pleasures of their own sins. Bodies that were made for the glory of God, abandoned to unnatural perversions; rotted with venereal diseases, ulcers, and sores; crippled and broken in a mad gamble with death just to "show off." Lungs designed to breathe God's pure air sentenced by cancer to wheeze and gasp; eyes and limbs created to do God's will made glazed and listless under the spell of drug addiction; various body parts temporarily disabled by the "hangover" of the morning after: the queasy stomach, the thudding head!

All these maladies we experience fulfill the Word of God: "Be not deceived; God is not mocked: for whatsoever [I repeat: *whatsoever*] a man soweth, that shall he also reap. For he that soweth to his flesh shall of the flesh reap corruption; but he that soweth to the Spirit shall of the Spirit reap life everlasting" (Gal. 6:7-8).

"Ye are not your own" (1 Cor. 6:19). *What* you do does not matter as much to God as *why* you do it! Ask yourself: Is it for God's glory? Will it exalt the truth?

Many seek God's grace, but *do they want His truth?* To receive it, they—all of us—must be willing to stop fighting God and surrender to Him unconditionally.

EIGHT

UNCONDITIONAL SURRENDER

I f you told me I was scheduled to fight in a fifteen-round contest against the world's champion boxer, I would find a convenient place to lie down at the feet of the referee and say, "Now then, Mr. Referee, please oblige me by counting me out quickly. I am no match for this opponent! Thank you!"

But some of us are not so wise when the opponent is God. We have tried fighting Him at our expense. Once engaged, we are like the Irishman in the following story: wanting to give up, but not knowing how to do it.

An ex-heavyweight boxer took a young Irishman in hand to train him. "Now, Paddy," he said, "when you have had enough, just cry out *Pax!* That means, 'Peace, I've had enough! I surrender.' Understand?" Paddy nodded. The two men went at it! If it had been a proper contest, round after round after round would have gone by. But with ripping, tearing, sledge-hammer blows, the two men, toe to toe, simply pounded one another until the ex-heavyweight could take no more and gasped out, "*Pax,*" as he collapsed on the floor.

Helping his trainer onto his feet, Paddy replied, "Shure bedad and that's the lovely wee word o'ive been trying to remember meself these last twenty minutes an' more!"

In contrast to the heavyweight, God doesn't give up when we engage Him. David says: "The Lord is my shepherd...He *maketh* me to lie down in green pastures" (Ps. 23:1-2, italics added). At times, it seems that the Lord has His hands full trying to make us lie down. But we are no match for Him. What a "lovely wee word" *pax,* or "I surrender," is! God has a way of getting us to say it, as the following story illustrates.

A rather large and ponderous lady who was married to a very thin and weedy little man was going out for the evening and had arranged for the babysitter to put all the children to bed. Upon returning, she asked the sitter how she had managed.

"Oh, no trouble, no trouble," she replied. "Except with the ginger-haired one, who came in after the others had gone to bed. He kicked and protested, but I settled him all right. I held his head under the cold water faucet until he gave in!"

"Oh," the good lady cried in dismay, "the ginger-haired one was my husband!"

Like the determined sitter, God always has a cold water faucet to "help" us give in. I learned this truth from personal experience.

"I Surrender"

In the early days of my ministry, 50 years ago, I would go to a place to run meetings and stay for perhaps a week. The people would come, and I would preach, and it was wonderful.

Then I pastored for 20 years in a church south of London. I was so fulfilled in that church! I *loved* it. I used to drive a big bus with a loudspeaker on the top, and I would put tapes on and then go around the villages like the Pied Piper of Hamlin, drawing the children in. I'd pack the old bus with 40 or more kids and take them to the church three times a week for children's meetings. We'd have Bible contests, stories, blackboard toffee competitions—you name it, we had it. I *loved* those kids.

I was involved with other church programs as well. Every Friday I took a group up to the Lambeth town hall in London; every Saturday I participated in outreaches; and every Sunday I conducted regular church services for the congregation. This, too, was wonderful.

Then all of a sudden, God said to me, "Go." I said, "No." A second time God said, "Go." But again I said, "No." After my second refusal, God didn't talk to me anymore; He began to deal with me. When He did, I learned something: the God of Jonah still lives! I realized that, in the whale's belly, Jonah was brought to a place where he would either *declare,* "Salvation is of the Lord," or (pardon the pun) *bewail,* "Salvation is of the Lord," one or the other. And in that place God began to deal with him.

That is the way it was with me. As a result of the Lord's "dealings," I was a dying man at age 51. I persisted in my disobedience for a time, but having my head under God's cold water faucet finally settled me. At two o'clock one morning, I surrendered to God. I said, "Lord, I'm going." He said, "Yes, you're going." I said, "But I had decided to stay!" God replied, "No, you're going. You'll either go and do what I've purposed you *should* do, or you're going home." Well, I knew I was saved, but I didn't want to be cut off, and I was facing that. So I surrendered to God, and in utter weakness, 34 years ago, I moved out.

I didn't go because I wanted to; I was pressurized into it. I was like the cowboy at the end of a tale I once read that went something like this:

An old prospector came down over the hills on a mule into a little sun-baked, western town. The old man dismounted and walked slowly across the road toward a drinking saloon. Just as he reached the entrance of the saloon, the swing doors opened, and out came a drunken cowboy with a Stetson on the back of his head and two guns in his hands. He was raring to go, looking for trouble. He fixed the old man in his sights and said with a slur, "Old man, did you ever dance?"

"No," said the old man, "I never did learn to dance. Life was too hard, son."

"Well," replied the cowboy, "you're sure going to dance today." And he took the two guns and started potting all around the old man's feet, so the old man had to quickly pick up his feet to avoid the bullets. The cowboy roared with laughter. Finally, all his ammunition was expended.

The old man turned his back on the cowboy, walked over to his mule, pulled a gun out of his saddle bag, lovingly handled it and pointed it at the cowboy's head. He said, "No, son, I sure never did learn to dance," and he swung the muzzle slowly around to just under the mule's tail, then back to the cowboy's head, then back again to just under the mule's tail.

"No, son," he repeated, "I sure never did learn to dance. But tell me something, son, did you ever kiss a mule *there?*"

The cowboy instantly sobered up. He looked at the old

man, his eyes big with fear, and said, "N-n-no! No, sir, I didn't, but...but I sure always *wanted* to!"

This story describes my response to God's dealings. I said in effect, "Lord, I never wanted to. But when you put the pistol to my head, I sure always wanted to." Whether you call it a whale's belly, a cold water faucet or a gun, God has a way of making us give in. How much easier if we just cooperate with Him in the first place!

Stop Fighting and Start Inviting

We need to stop fighting God and start inviting Him into our failures. If sin is a consequence and not a cause, if pride (man's glory) is the cause of our sins, then we ought to stop dusting the cobweb down and use the cobweb to catch the spider!

When we have truth in the inward parts—the truth about our sins—God will use the sins to break the pride. You may be very fond of strawberries and cream, but if God puts mustard on the strawberries, you will very soon lose your desire for them! From the inside God will begin to break your failure into small pieces by the entrance of truth until it dissolves in the light. The hymn-writer says, "Search me, O God, my actions try, and *let my life appear as seen by thine all-searching eye.* To me my ways make clear."

Stop fighting and start inviting! When you do, you will have truth.

I read the following little ditty on a postcard I once came across at the seaside: "Tobacco is a hateful weed: I like it! It makes you thin, it makes you lean, it takes the hair right off your bean; it's the worst darned stuff I've ever seen, but I like it!" The man who wrote this ditty has a problem; he loves something he ought to hate. What should he do? Having truth splits the problem up!

The devil cannot operate in truth. He "abode not in

the truth, because there is no truth in him" (John 8:44). He is as helpless in truth as a shark in a parking lot. The shark needs his natural environment—water—to function normally. The devil needs his environment to function, also, and it is always some form of lie: bluffs, counterfeits, mirages, forgeries, delusions, vain imaginations, masks—in short, anything that is not real. You name it, Satan has it!

Everything the devil offers is a clever counterfeit of the real. *True* but not *truth!*

On each chain the devil uses to bind men up, there is always one link that isn't real. Which one is that? The first! He is a liar from the beginning (John 8:44). Examine the first link that binds you in your failure and you will find that you are believing a lie. It is not the truth! Pride is always built on a lie.

Many a woman who is divorced from a husband she once loved has a problem. The court awarded her the custody of the children but gave the husband the legal right to visit them. She wants the children but hates the father. However, she cannot keep the father away from the children because she had them when in union with him. If she does not want the father, she must relinquish the custody of the children.

The Scriptures tell us that the devil is the father of the lie (John 8:44). That makes the lie the child of the devil. God will uphold the legal right of the devil to visit his own. Jesus claimed, "The prince of this world cometh, and hath nothing in me" (John 14:30). Why did Satan have nothing in Him? Because Jesus is the *truth!* He Himself said, "I am the way, the truth, and the life" (John 14:6). Thus the man who abides in Jesus is devil-proof!

Our problem is that we listen to the plausible lies of the devil, who promises us all sorts of things if we will serve him. Then, like the prodigal son, we end up in the pig-swill of disillusionment with the realization that our heavenly Father treats His hired servants better than we are being treated; in fact, He treats them almost like sons. They "have bread enough *and to spare*." They are not desperately waiting for pay-day; they have some left over. Yet "[we] perish with hunger!" (See Luke 15:11-32, esp. v. 17.)

The man who believes a lie is fighting both God *and* the devil. Let me repeat: God will uphold the legal right of the devil to visit his own! Truth in the inward parts will dissolve the platform of lies upon which your failure stands. Call the devil's bluff. Then watch God!

If you have a problem, instead of fighting God start inviting God. Watch it break from the inside as you receive truth.

Unconditional Surrender

Some people have ceased fighting God, but they haven't yet learned to invite Him into their situation. Like the warring countries at the end of World War I, they have signed an armistice with God in the railway carriage of their own choosing. They are officially no longer at war with Him because they have come to "terms."

After the Nazi uprising under Hitler during the Second World War, the only "terms" the western nations would accept was unconditional surrender. The insistence on complete surrender was preceded by 1,000 bomber raids on German territory—blockbusters on the marshalling yard of Hamburg. Night after night, waves of Lancaster bombers brought death and destruction to the might of the German empire. The continual attacks finally culminated at Hiroshima, Japan, with the awful horror of the atom bomb.

This intentional, extensive destruction was called a "softening up" process. After the smoke and dust had cleared from the twisted, mutilated mass of humanity, a shocked and shaken world was ushered, dazed and subdued, into a new era. Conquered and conqueror alike were made strangely aware of the terrifying import of the day of fullness.

Now what does this mean to you and me?

The two wars are typical of the internal struggle that goes on in the life of the believer. World War I, which ended with "terms," obviously speaks of measure, whereas World War II, which terminated with the unconditional surrender of the enemy, is representative of fullness. The enemy at the end of the second major conflict was completely destroyed: "terms" were done away with; the Nazi party was exterminated; and Hitler was annihilated.

Here's the analogy. All of us by nature are at enmity with God; in other words, at war. We have been "reconciled" through our Lord Jesus Christ to the Father, and most believers have come to "terms," or made an armistice, with Him.

But few of us know anything about unconditional surrender to God because this involves the complete destruction of the "government." The "party" must lose its identity; the uprising must be totally squelched by the abdication of my heart from the throne. This is fullness! After the Second World War, the Nazi party was dissolved; it had no function in fullness but to lose its identity in unconditional surrender. In like manner, my personality—my "self"—is to be eclipsed in the blaze of the glory of God. Surrender without a condition!

The Scriptures tell us that the government is upon *His* shoulder (not ours), and that of the increase of His government and peace, *there shall be no end* (see Is. 9:6). But are we willing to step down and let Him rule and reign in our hearts in order for these Scriptures to be fulfilled? Do we know what this requires?

With so much of the world in revival, it seems that wherever I go, I hear people calling for the fire of God.

"Oh, God, send the fire!" they cry. But do they realize what the fire does? The fire searches. The fire burns. The fire causes loss of identity. In the fire, everything that is not of God gets consumed. If you are committed to the fire, you can't negotiate with the flames!

In his day (the day of measure) John rightly said, "[Christ] must increase...I must decrease" (John 3:30), but in line with the day of fullness I no longer exist at all. Acts 17:30 declares that there was a time when God winked at our ignorance, and Paul implies that he was permitted a measure of self-exaltation regarding the abundance of revelations he had received, because he says he was given a thorn in the flesh, "Lest [he] should be exalted *above* measure" (2 Cor. 12:7, italics added). In the day of fullness, however, no flesh will be permitted to glory *at all* in His presence (1 Cor. 1:29).

The time for a complete eviction order has arrived! "Now the Lord had said unto Abram, Get thee out of thy country" (Gen. 12:1). It's time for *us* to *get out!* In order to be filled with God, we must be emptied of ourselves.

Are we willing? Are we ready to lay everything on the altar for God?

Jesus was. In the garden of Gethsemane, He faced the biggest battle of His life: whether or not to die for you. He didn't want to do it. He said, "Oh, Father, let this cup pass from me. I don't want to drink it." But when His Father did not remove the cup, Jesus submitted. He said, "Nevertheless, Father, not My will, but Thine be done" (see Matt. 26:39). And you know the outcome of His decision; unconditional surrender took Him to the cross in our stead.

I Can of Mine Own Self Do Nothing

In the day of measure there is a place for me to be a coworker with God and, like Paul, I may cry, "I can do all things through Christ which strengtheneth me"

74

(Phil. 4:13). Yet the Son of God, who operated in fullness, declares, "I can of mine own self do nothing...; [it is] the Father that dwelleth in me, he doeth the works" (John 5:30; 14:10).

God is all in all! The Lord Jesus has an "Himself," a "Me," a personality that does not operate on His own. "I can of mine own [Him]self do nothing; as I hear, I judge" (John 5:30). He is subject! Similarly, the Holy Spirit has an "Himself," a "Me," a personality that does not operate on His own. "He shall not speak *of himself*; but whatsoever he shall hear, that shall he speak" (John 16:13, italics added). He, too, is subject!

In the Trinity there are three speakers and three doers, but the Son and the Spirit are also listeners. God the Father is all in all or, if you like, all in three. "Of Him" are all things! So then in fullness, neither the Son nor the Holy Spirit do anything of themselves. Only One operates in the Trinity—the Father! Now we see the significance of Jesus' words, "The Father that dwelleth in me, *he* doeth the works" (John 14:10, italics added). They point to the secret of the mystery of God: *If the glory is all God's, then the work is all God's!*

Thus the responsibility of my "himself" is to "let go and let God"—to get out of the way—my only struggle, a struggle *not* to struggle! As David said when he stood before the towering Goliath, "The battle is the Lord's" (1 Sam. 17:47).

I am not called to a life of inactivity, but rather to a life of active service as a yielded channel of God's divine power. Jesus declared He could do nothing and then did everything, by the power of another substitution. His was no negative confession of defeat, but rather the triumphant cry of one who was jealous for His Father's glory.

He claimed, "Though *of My own self* I can do nothing, *all power* is given unto Me" (see John 5:30; Matt. 28:18). He stilled the storms, raised the dead, vanished sickness,

rebuked demons and multiplied food so superlatively
that He had more left over after feeding a crowd of thousands than He had when He started.

In the day of fullness, we are to operate like Jesus
did, doing nothing of ourselves and yet doing everything. This is our birthright, our destiny! The only reason we can't lay hold of it is that we are filled up with
ourselves.

God's Softening Up Process

To return to the illustration of the two wars: How
many believers have come to "terms" with God, instead
of unconditionally surrendering to Him in their hearts?
God has a measure of glory for the measure of work He
has been permitted to do in a life.

Presently, God is endeavoring to bring some of us to
the point of surrender. We have been subject to heavenly air raids; God has been dropping bombs on the forti-
fications of the empire of our flesh life. Blockbusters
with unerring precision have devastated our communi-
cation lines, and many of us have been made aware that
we are in a preparatory "softening up" process. Like
Saul on the Damascus road, bewildered and perplexed
if not in despair, we have cried out, asking, "Who art
thou, Lord?" (Acts 9:5).

The preparation of the heart is of the Lord, and the
counsel and the work go together (Is. 28:29). God offers all
His fullness to those who are prepared to offer Him all
their emptiness. Are you willing to give up all for Jesus?

NINE

THE DIVINE PLAN

J ean Paul Richter once declared, "The crucified Jew, being the mightiest among the holy, and the holiest among the mighty, has with His pierced hands, lifted empires off their hinges, turned the stream of centuries and *still* governs the ages!"

The long-lasting and world-wide impact Jesus has had on society cannot be ignored by either believer or infidel; both are compelled to pay homage as they ask to be put off the bus in front of a famous cathedral such as St. Paul's, and with the coin they tender, they must acknowledge His birthday, for it is dated A.D.—*anno Domini*—the year of our Lord. They may get drunk at Christmas and Easter, but at least admit that it is His birthday and His resurrection that give them the excuse to do it!

How much more can we add to testify to this unknown Nazarene who emerged from a carpenter's shop? The dumb, the deaf, the lame, the blind, the leper—even the humble little fish with a coin in its mouth—all hasten to pay homage to Jesus! Many, many millions of us, at this moment, are hailing "the power of Jesus' name!"

What does His existence mean to us? Stripped of all sentiment and fine language, what is the basic truth that Jesus came to reveal? Simply this: The Father, for the glory of His Name, will never be satisfied with anything less than the fulfillment of His divine plan, which was declared in the beginning. God *must* have the last word, and the *first* word will be the *last* word. "Let us make man in our image, after our likeness: and let them have dominion...over all the earth" (Gen. 1:26).

Imputed Versus Imparted Righteousness

Jesus came to redeem man out of the devil's pawnshop, not with silver or gold but with His precious blood (see 1 Pet. 1:18). "By one offering he hath perfected for ever them that are sanctified" (Heb. 10:14). "We are sanctified through the offering of the body of Jesus Christ once for all" (Heb. 10:10).

"Perfected for ever...once for all." What is the secret of a perfect, or uttermost, salvation? One word: *substitution.* What does it mean? "In the stead of." The perfect, sinless Man died in the place of the imperfect, sinful man. So I am justified in the sight of God *just as if* I'd never sinned! Christ died for (instead of) me. I am represented by proxy! Therefore, I stand complete in Him. I have an *imputed* righteousness until I have an *imparted* righteousness. The scaffolding around a building remains until the building is finished!

"By so much was Jesus made the surety of a better testament [covenant, arrangement]" (Heb. 7:22). He is my assurance in the time of uncertainty. He ever lives to make intercession. He stands in the gap for me. He not only pays my debt in the hour when I am up for unpaid debts, but He is heaven's loan, standing bail until my case comes up for trial. The hymn-writer says (and I believe it), "*All* the worth I have before Him is the value of the blood!"

You have no righteousness of your own, yet you are complete in Him. As the scaffolding goes up before the building, so you have an imputed righteousness before an imparted righteousness. The following interchange between two young girls helps to illustrate the meaning of these terms.

1st little girl: "How many pennies do you have, Jennifer?"

2nd little girl: "I have five pennies."

1st little girl: "I have ten pennies!"

2nd little girl: "Let me see. Oh, you little fibber, you have only five, same as me!"

1st little girl: "No, I haven't; I have ten!"

2nd little girl: "You can't count; you have the same as me!"

1st little girl: "Yes, I can count. Listen, this morning when my daddy went out, he asked me, 'Mary, how many pennies do you have?' I said, 'Five, Daddy.' And he said, 'When I come in tonight, I'll double your pennies!' So, there. I have ten pennies!"

The first little girl reckoned her daddy's words were the words of a gentleman, and she chose to believe what he said rather than what she saw. The pennies were *imputed* to her before they were *imparted* to her!

Which do you believe: your experience, your opinions, your feelings, what your body tells you or *what God says?* God has put us and placed us and made us and, while it does not yet fully appear, it will—"when Daddy comes home tonight"! "For all the promises of God in him [Jesus Christ] are yea, and in him Amen, unto the glory of God" (2 Cor. 1:20).

Conformed to the Image of the Son

In an uttermost salvation there will be those with an imparted righteousness who are conformed to the image of the Son, that He might be "the firstborn among many brethren" (Rom. 8:29). The Bible says that this is our destiny! "For whom [God] did foreknow, he also did predestinate to be conformed to the image of His Son" (Rom. 8:29). *Whom He did foreknow.* That's us! *He did predestinate.* He ordained it! It's His plan for us to be an extension of Himself.

Jesus is the only begotten of the Father, but He is the firstborn of many brethren (see John 1:14,18; 3:16; Rom. 8:29). His death and resurrection made a way for us to become children of God. "As many as received [Jesus], to them gave he power to become the sons of God, even to them that believe on his name: Which were born, not of blood, nor of the will of the flesh, nor of the will of man, but of God" (John 1:12-13). Those who are born of the Spirit are *the sons,* Jesus' brethren, and the purpose of God is that they should be conformed to the image of *the Son.*

Whatever you see in the Son is the purpose for the sons. Ephesians 4:13 says, "till we all come...unto a perfect man, unto the measure of the stature of the fulness of Christ."

What does this mean? That God will have other sons as big as Jesus! Do you realize that everything Jesus did, and even greater works, *must be done in other* sons, for God's original purpose to be fulfilled? *God* (not Satan and not man) *must have the last word!* God's glory is at stake (Num. 14:21).

The world has *yet* to see the manifestation of the sons

of God! This is the full bloom of a "much more" salvation, to the credit—the glory—of God. The purpose of this uttermost salvation is that by *one* Spirit, in *one* hope, *one* faith and *one* baptism, as *one* body we shall all be made *one* in Christ Jesus, who is *one* with the Father!

Just before He died, Jesus prayed for His disciples that they might be one as He and the Father are one (John 17:11). He understood that once the "other sons," including all of us, received the principle of the first Son, they would live like Him. Man is a triune being, and when God said "Let us make man in our image, after our likeness," He purposed to be all in all, to fill all three parts of us—body, soul and spirit (Gen. 1:26). Paul told the Corinthians, "When that which is perfect [God] is come, then that which is in part [you] shall be done away" (1 Cor. 13:10). We are "the fulness of Him that filleth all in all" (Eph. 1:23).

Jesus declared, "I and my Father are one" (John 10:30). No division. If you are to be conformed to the image of the Son, you also will cry, "I and my Father are one!"

As We Are One

How are we to be one with the Father? *As* Jesus is one with the Father! We must understand the "as," because that's how it's got to be for us. As *He* is, so are *we*. The only way it's ever going to work for the sons is the way it works between the Father and the Son. How are they one?

Let me give you a comparison. Looking out of a window, I notice that the glass is totally transparent. I can see through it with no difficulty. It is just as if the window isn't there, unless condensation, steam, dust or fly dirt coat and soil it. If it is perfectly clean, the glass is utterly transparent. That's how it is with Jesus. And that's how it is to be with us. The purpose of God for our lives is that it be *just as if we're not there.*

81

Shortly before Jesus died, Philip said to Him, "Lord, shew us the Father, and it sufficeth us." Jesus was almost astonished. He replied, "Have I been so long time with you, and yet hast thou not known me, Philip? he that hath seen me hath seen the Father" (John 14:8-9). Jesus could say this in truth because He is the total, absolute expression of the Father.

Have you ever heard a person, while looking at a baby, say, "Oh, he's just like his daddy! Same old ginger hair. Same funny little nose. Just like his daddy!" People could rightfully say of Jesus, "Just like His Father." Won't it be a day to rejoice when people can look at the other sons and use the same expression to describe us?

While Jesus was on earth, He ministered the presence of Another. He had an Himself that didn't operate. This is the pattern for us. *"As* We are one."

How does the principle of oneness with God, or fullness, operate in a person? To answer this question, let's look at Mary, the mother of Jesus. When Elizabeth greeted her after she had conceived Jesus, Mary said, "*My soul* doth magnify the Lord, and *my spirit* hath rejoiced in God my Saviour" (Luke 1:46-47, italics added). This statement indicates that two parts of Mary's being, soul and spirit, were filled with God.

Later, when Jesus told her that He must be about His Father's business, Mary "understood not the saying" but kept it "*in her heart*" (Luke 2:49-51, italics added). With the heart man believes! So three parts of Mary—soul, spirit and heart in a body—were at one with God.

The fullness of God—"the measure of the stature of the fullness of Christ"—demands all! But it is not some rare, to-be-hoped-for experience; it's your birthright! It's offered to you; it's open to you. Don't settle for less by hanging on to yourself. If you are willing to lose your identity in the Holy Spirit, the Holy Spirit will form and extend the image of the Son in you.

The Order of God

Jesus will never be satisfied until there are others who can say in truth, like He did, "I and my Father are one" (John 10:30). He will never be satisfied until He sees the travail of His soul in His brethren (Is. 53:11). He said, "I will build my church; and *the gates of hell shall not prevail against it*" (Matt. 16:18, italics added). He must finish the job Father has given Him to do!

When He has done so, there will be others like Himself whose lives come into order—the order of God— instead of disorder. In an ordered life, everything—salvation, healing, deliverance, blessing and so on—is prioritized in such a way that the glory of God takes precedence. The glory of God alone has first place.

May I close this chapter with a children's story about order? Once upon a time there was a million dollars. Now this million dollars was made up of a unit (a one) and six zeros. The unit was first and was everything, and the six zeros followed and were nothing, but strangely enough, in the proper order, the unit added such value to the zeros that, with it, they made a million dollars.

Each little zero in its order had value and also increased the value of the one. "My strength is made perfect in weakness" (2 Cor. 12:9). But one day there was trouble!

The last zero said, "I'm fed up with always being last; I am like the cow's tail, forever behind. I want a change; I'm going to move!" So he moved! He pushed himself up to the front and landed here $01,000,00. Now, because he was "out" of order, he was worth nothing, and the million dollars became a hundred thousand dollars, like this: $100,000.

But that was not all; when the other little zeros saw what he had done, they became discontented and wanted to move too! So they did. The former million dollars now looked like this: $000,000,1. The zeros discovered that they were of value only when they were in order *after* the one. They became good for nothing because they were *out of order!* Wrong order reduced one million dollars to one dollar.

Have you ever gone up to a vending machine hoping to buy a snack, only to find a notice on the machine which reads, "Out of Order"? The sign indicates that the machine is of no use. This is the great tragedy of man's life: He is often of no use to God because he is out of order!

The only proper order is for God's glory to be number one. Thus, *the lost key of the universe is the Father's glory in my heart.* Thine is the glory!

"Thine is the glory" is safe in the heart that is yoked to Jesus, who says, "Take *My* yoke upon you" (Matt. 11:29, italics added).

Be All God Intended You to Be

It is so sad when people fail to become all that they were meant to become. You were *born* to be conformed to the image of Jesus! You were born to come into the measure of the stature of the fullness of Christ! You were born to be the extension of God! Don't let the failures you've experienced keep you from your destiny, like the man who describes himself in this poem:

I think my life is a tame old duck
dibbling around in the farmyard muck,
fat and lazy with useless wings!
But sometimes when the north wind sings
and the wild ducks hurtle overhead,
something stirs that was lost and dead,
And it cocks a wary and puzzled eye
and makes a feeble attempt to fly!
It's fairly content with the state it's in,
But it's not the duck it might have been!

A tame old duck with useless wings! Does this describe your life?

When the storm comes, most birds cower and hide, but the eagle does not seek shelter from the storm; with a piercing scream, it flies into the tempest and is lifted above it! Other birds flap up. The eagle mounts up! On a lone crag he waits for a current of air and mounts up with ease. Isaiah 40:31 declares, "They that wait upon the Lord shall renew their strength; they shall *mount up* with wings as eagles" (italics added).

My friend in failure, the wind of God has come to your crag. Spread your wings and, as the Spirit of Truth blows, embrace the truth and rise on it, into the presence of God. You will become the eagle God intended you to be—a son in the image of the Son—rather than a tame old duck with useless wings.

TEN

RETURN TO THE GARDEN

Strange as it may seem, man goes everywhere to deal with his troubles except to the source, or the place where things went wrong. What motorist with a puncture in his back wheel would pull out the plug to rectify his troubles? Who goes to the dentist when he has a sprained ankle? We need to remember that the law of cause and effect is inexorable; if we don't deal with the cause, we will suffer the effect.

In the beginning, God gave man *one* command and *one* command only. That commandment has never been rescinded! "Of the tree of the knowledge of good and evil, thou shalt not eat of it: for in the day that thou eatest thereof thou shalt surely die" (Gen. 2:17).

The first commandment is still the first commandment! Notice that God refers to the *tree*, not the *trees*, of the knowledge of good and evil. One and the same tree produces two fruits, and it is not only the fruit of the knowledge of evil that is forbidden to man, but the fruit of the entire tree.

What does this mean? It means that, from the beginning, *the knowledge of good* was forbidden to man. The reason? Out of my knowledge of good comes my knowledge of evil!

If I do not know the first, I cannot know the second. Therefore, if I do not eat of the tree, I do not know, and if I do not know, I cannot judge. Jesus said, "Judge not that ye be not judged" (Matt. 7:1).

If I refuse to eat, I find myself in the ideal situation of helplessness that Jesus described when He declared, "I can of mine own self do nothing: as I hear, I judge" (John 5:30). He did not say as I *eat*, but as I *hear!* He got His direction from the Father's voice. Unless His Father spoke to Him, He did not know, because He had never eaten of the tree.

Jesus said that man should live by every word that proceedeth out of the mouth of God (Matt. 4:4). The vital difference between sons and slaves—the sons of God and the slaves of Satan—is that sons hear and obey the will of the Father. "As many as are led by the Spirit of God, they are the sons of God" (Roms. 8:14). The sons wax strong in spirit as they are led, and they are led as they *listen,* not as they *eat!*

The slaves, on the other hand, listen to their master Satan, and as they eat of the tree, they are tied to its bondage! Their eating of the forbidden fruit is not equivalent to a small boy's escapade of snitching apples from the farmer's field; no, this tree is inside you! Every time man eats of the tree of the knowledge of good and evil and from that knowledge pronounces a judgement, he breaks the first commandment of God and partakes of death! Guidance by the Spirit will come only to the man who refuses to eat of the tree.

I may see *what* you do—that is merely an observation—but I do not know *why* you do it. I have no idea what your motive is; hence I cannot judge you. From the moment that I know what is good, I presume that I know what is evil. This presumption is the seat of man's glory and the enemy of the glory of God! You will find that it is the launching platform of *all* your troubles! Deal with this, and you deal with the lot!

The greater includes the lesser! No need to keep the Ten Commandments. Keep the first ("Thou shalt not eat of it"), and you will keep the ten!

Man's pride is always born out of what he knows, his self-exaltation out of what he thinks is good. When tremblingly Adam said to his Maker, "I was naked; and I hid myself," God responded with the question, "Who told thee that thou wast naked?" In other words, where did you get your information? "Hast thou eaten of the tree, whereof I commanded thee that thou shouldest not eat?" (Gen. 3:10-11).

True Versus Truth

When a man goes the devil's way and eats of the tree, he will know what is *true* but never the *truth.* He is deceived because he accepts what is true in place of the truth. His knowledge of good becomes the enemy of God just as the good, and not the worst, is the enemy of the best.

To illustrate: Many of my friends have heard me say, "In all the times I stopped at so and so's house, they never gave me a cup of tea!" This is true, and, of course, makes my host and hostess appear very inhospitable, but the truth is, I do not drink tea!

During the war between England and France in the

early 1800's, Vice Admiral Horatio Nelson of the British Navy was directed to attack a Danish fleet at Copenhagen. However, after Nelson's superior assessed the strength of the enemy ships, he signaled Nelson to retreat. The Vice Admiral put a telescope to his blind eye and studied the signal. Not wanting to obey his orders, he declared to an aide, "I really do not see the signal."

What Nelson said was true but not the truth. He could have seen the Admiral's signal if he had wanted to. There is no deception in truth, but men will lie with what is *true* and use it to conceal the *truth!* For example, we are two hours late to an appointment because we were lazy and laid in bed too long (the truth), but we explain our late arrival by the fact that we had a puncture on the road (which is true). The flat tire did not make us two hours overdue; we changed it in less than ten minutes!

I knew a woman who would say to her husband each evening, "I'm taking Pinky for a walk" (Pinky was the pet poodle). Her husband would grunt from the depths of the evening paper or from in front of the television, the door would shut and she would be gone. What she said was true: She did take Pinky for a walk, but she used what was true to hide the truth. She was meeting another man every night!

Then there is the old, old excuse of the husband who is kept late at the office—fortunately for him, his wife can only *hear* him over the phone and not *see* him. "Sorry, Dear, my hands are so full with things at the office, I won't be home until eight!" His hands are full all right—with coffee and biscuits—and his arms, too—with the typist, as he sits cuddling her! The demands of "business" have delayed him!

Think of the cunning salesman, who insists, "Yes, madam; this is definitely the last one!" It is—until he opens another box! What he claims is so true, but it is not the truth. Or the enterprising shopkeeper with the box on the counter marked "FOR THE BLIND." When it is filled by the generous donations of his philanthropic customers, he buys himself a new window blind!

The little apple, the false smile, the thought you think but never say, the motive that *launched* the act. Not the *what,* but the *why!* The lie you tell by keeping your mouth shut! Putting forward what is true as a substitute for truth to conceal the truth. Using twenty words to "slither down" when five God-given words would "bring you down." Only three words make an apology: *I was wrong!*

Covering and cloaking in pretense! The extra industrious effort as the foreman or the teacher enters. Pretending to wipe your nose while you are looking at a pretty girl's legs. Looking in a shop window to get the reflection of someone across the road while you act as if you haven't seen him. Sitting with your back to the light so that the pimples on your face don't show up.

All of us hide behind what is true: You have done it; I have done it; the devil does it. Only deceivers are deceived!

If there is one thing worse than bad eggs labeled "bad eggs," it is bad eggs labeled "good eggs"! While the devil abides not in the truth, he is quite at home juggling what is true. Even the Word of God can be handled deceitfully!

Well, so what? Maybe we know something about these things for the same reason that the old huntsman knows the crack of the whip: because he is familiar with the sound! One thing is definite, "[God] desirest *truth* [not just what is true] in the inward parts" (Ps. 51:6, italics added).

Oh, God make me real! If I am only a nickel or a dime, don't let me pose as a quarter or a half dollar!

Return to the Garden

The truth will never magnify man because it is not the glory of man, but the glory of God. In our search for the lost key, we need to go back to the garden of Eden because that is where it was lost. Only where man lost it will he find it. Once man made a choice to know.

Satan was there to supply him with all the information he needed, and apparently it was true information that fed his reason. "Ye shall not surely die...ye shall be as gods, knowing good and evil" (Gen. 3:4-5).

It is *true* that Adam went on living physically after he ate of the tree. But the *truth* is that in the day that he ate of it, Adam died to God in his soul and was dead while he lived! His descendants are born in the same condition, because "in Adam *all* die" (1 Cor. 15:22, italics added). When we come into the world, we are "dead in trespasses and in sins" (Eph. 2:1). All men must therefore be *born again:* "In Christ shall all be made alive" (1 Cor. 15:22).

Man will never know dominion except in the realm where he lost it—the other side of the tree!

Years ago I was lost in a maze at Hampton Court Palace. I remember looking up and seeing someone in a box, high above me, pointing the way. This experience reminds me of what man is like today.

Ever since God evicted Adam from the garden of Eden "lest he...take also of the tree of life, and eat, and live for ever" and placed "at the east of the garden...a flaming sword which turned every way, to keep the way of the tree of life," man has been confused, like someone who is seeking the way and is confronted with a signpost that swings aimlessly any way the wind blows (Gen. 3:22-24). Without the Holy Spirit, he continues to wander aimlessly in his bewildered state. The Holy Spirit alone will guide man into *all truth* (revelation) so that he can find his way back into dominion in the garden.

No one will ever climb up some other way than by the way of truth (see John 10:1). Jesus said, "I thank Thee, O Father, Lord of heaven and earth, because thou hast hid these things from the wise and prudent, and hast revealed them unto babes. Even so, Father: for so it seemed good in thy sight" (Matt. 11:25-26).

God is working to bring us back into the garden, to dominion, to "the measure of the stature of the fulness of Christ" (Eph. 4:13). We are to be as big as Jesus, to be conformed to the image of the Son that He might be the firstborn among many brethren (Rom. 8:29). He *shall* see of the travail of His soul and be satisfied (Is. 53:11).

Greater works than His shall *ye* do! Oh, dear reader, do you see it? Has God's Holy Spirit shown you the lost key? Has the eternal plan been revealed to you? If not, humble yourself now and ask God to reveal it. The words are in this little book, but only the mighty Spirit of God can quicken and impart revelation; I cannot.

Only in the life where "Thine is the glory" is wrought will the work of transformation be done and dominion be given. They said of Jesus, "What manner of man is this! for he commandeth even the winds and water, and they obey him" (Luke 8:25). God's plan will never be fulfilled until even greater works are done in the second body of Jesus Christ, which is His church and of which you are members in particular. These works will bring even greater glory to His great name.

If you are the father of a little boy, you feed him, clothe him, correct him, love him and do everything else that is required to bring him to maturity, to the fullness of manhood. At times it may be expedient for you to leave him so that you can go to work to provide the money to make caring for him possible—until the day when he reaches fullness. At that time, his accomplishments may exceed your own. I myself have sons who are "bigger" than I am. Jesus told His disciples, "Greater works than these shall ye do!" (See John 14:12.)

Led by the Spirit

To fulfill the divine plan, some must attain to the measure of the stature of the fullness of Christ. Have *you* begun the journey yet? It is recorded of Jesus that he "waxed strong in spirit" (Luke 1:80; 2:40); to grow to full stature, we must, also.

"As many as are *led* by the Spirit of God, they are the sons of God" (Rom. 8:14, italics added). Are you led by the Spirit? "It is the *spirit* that quickeneth" (John 6:63, italics added). "Not by *might*, nor by *power*, but *by my spirit*, saith the Lord!" (Zech. 4:6, italics and emphasis added). You cannot ride to Australia via land, but in another realm—that of the air—you may soar above earth and sea and arrive. The greater works and the fullness of Christ are possible *only* in the realm of the Spirit, not in the realm of the flesh. Not in the realm of the soul! You are equipped for this flight. God has given you a spirit. He has also given you a Pilot—the Holy Spirit—to guide you into *all* truth. The Pilot will show you how the "joy stick" and all the other "controls" operate.

I once heard a brother describe a flight he had taken over the Himalayan Mountains. At a particular moment, the pilot announced, "You are now looking down at the highest point in the world—the top of Mount Everest!" The brother gazed down with a strange awe upon the grim rock that reared its head up from the midst of the snowy slopes and mused upon the many lives that had been lost or endangered as they sought to conquer this peak of all peaks. He considered in contrast the ease and comfort with which he looked down upon what other men had struggled to climb up to. The contrast between this brother's experience and that of the struggling mountain climbers contains a parable for us.

The strivings of the flesh and the conflicts of the soul will never take us to the God-like realm of the Spirit where nothing is impossible, where our mountains and our valleys cease to be. We cannot get there by "land"; we must get "airborne"!

Buy the Truth

So much for the blueprint—the vision—now for the practical application. We have window-gazed long enough at every shop; now to spend our money, to buy the truth! What does it cost? Get your purse out! No man can go the way of the Spirit without humbling himself and submitting to the Spirit of God! He is the Spirit of truth, the essence of reality. How can two walk together, except they be agreed? (see Amos 3:3). Whatever is sham, vanity, unreality, living to man and so on must go.

Remember, you do not ask God to deliver you from your pride; you *humble yourself* (see 1 Pet. 5:5). Admittedly, you must do it under the mighty hand, but you do it! Go to it! God will show you the counter where you can buy the truth (no good attempting to buy a cauliflower at the clothing store).

"But," you ask, "with what do I buy?" If you are going the Spirit's way, you will have to pay with your pride. Pride, man's glory, is a lie. God's glory comes in as yours goes out! In other words, humbling is a way of life. You continually bow and humble *to* God but *before* man.

Continually bowing, continually humbling oneself, continually giving God *all* the glory is the lost key!

In every situation in life, you will choose to either (1) exalt yourself as you eat of the forbidden tree of the knowledge of good (and automatically of evil), thus becoming your own god ("Knowledge puffeth up," 1 Cor. 8:1) and judging from what you know; or (2) humble yourself and refuse to eat of the forbidden tree, consequently abiding in a place where you do not know and hence cannot judge.

If you choose to humble yourself, you will be reduced to a state of utter helplessness: "I don't know!" But it is when you are in this state that you will "attain to...the fullness of Christ," for since you do not know, you *must* have a proceeding word from the mouth of God. and the Spirit will ultimately lead you past the flaming sword back into the garden, back into dominion, back to the original purpose of God (Eph. 4:13; Matt. 4:4).

This man (you) must operate as *that* man (Jesus)

operated! I repeat: *must*, not *may*. Christ was the only man who ever lived normally.

When we are living normally, the miracle of yesterday becomes the commonplace of today. How? By an increase of revelation! Henry VIII's eyes would have nearly popped out at the sight of a T.V. set, but not the child of today; he takes it as a matter of course. The miraculous will be a matter of course for the sons, because they will say, as Jesus did:

"I am able to do nothing from Myself [independently, of My Own accord—but only as I am taught by God and as I get His orders]. Even as I hear, I judge [I decide as I am bidden to decide. As the voice comes to Me, so I give a decision], and My judgment is right (just, righteous), because I do not seek or consult My own will [I have no desire to do what is pleasing to Myself, My own aim, My own purpose] but *only* the will and pleasure of the Father Who sent Me" (John 5:30, AMP, italics added).

Because Jesus did not eat, He decides as He is *bidden to decide.* Do you see this? *As* the voice (of God) comes to me, so I give a decision! As I hear, I judge! This is the way the Son of God ticks! It must be the way the other sons operate, also.

Why We Fail

We are meant to function as Jesus did, being directed by the voice of God. Nevertheless, we fail. It is not because we are weak that we sin or fall, else Jesus would have been the biggest sinner of all! He freely admitted that He was weak when He said, "I can of My own Self do nothing." We fail because God removes the grace that holds us up! Why does God remove the grace? Because, in our pride, we do not give Him the glory for it. We need grace for grace (John 1:16). God has no grace for pride.

Where is my pride? My pride is located in my judgments, which come out of my knowledge of good, which I have obtained by deliberately disobeying God in eating of the tree of the knowledge of good and evil in the hidden man of the heart! I am permitted to observe but not to judge!

What is the difference? I observe *what* you do. I do not know *why* you do it. Therefore I must not judge you, unless God supernaturally gives me spiritual judgment (often called discernment) not based on the tree. That is heavenly judgment! A scriptural example: Peter asks Ananias, "Why has Satan filled thine heart to lie to the Holy Ghost?" Peter had no way of knowing, except by the Holy Spirit, that Ananias was pretending to give all the money from the sale of his property while withholding part of it (see Acts 5:1-3). God gave Peter the insight because He wanted to reveal Ananias's deceitfulness.

All judgment other than spiritual discernment is wrong. "Judge not, that ye be not judged" (Matt. 7:1). When you judge, you father your failure! "Thou that judgest *doest the same things*" (Rom. 2:1, italics added). You dig your own grave when you judge!

Eating of the Tree

As a boil indicates an unseen condition in which the blood is out of order because of a poor diet, so your judgments reveal an unseen condition in which your life is out of order because of a poor diet! This wrong diet consists in eating of the tree instead of listening to the voice. "Man [does] not live by bread alone, but by every word that proceedeth out of the mouth of God" (Matt. 4:4). Calories aren't everything!

In the natural, wrong diet produces a disorder that affects the blood stream. One of the symptoms of this disorder is the appearance on the skin of boils filled with poison called pus! In the spiritual, wrong diet (eating of the tree) also produces a disorder that results in boils. My judgments are my spiritual boils filled with pus! These the blood does not cleanse. The blood of Jesus avails for my sin but not for my pride (1 Pet. 5:5-6).

As a young man I suffered much with boils—on my head, my neck, my arms, my legs. I once had a carbuncle on my knee with five heads on it!

One day I was talking to a friend of mine who was a chemist, and he suggested that I try a certain paste that would draw the poison out. This remedy would save me all the misery of steam poultices and the pushing, pressing and squeezing that up to then had been my lot.

I tried the paste, and it worked! Henceforth I went out like a crusader against boils. I was excited; I told everybody I met who suffered with boils about "my remedy" and how it had worked for me.

One day I was in the house of a miner. He was stripped to the waist, lying groaning across the table while his wife and daughter applied boiling fomentations to four or five huge, ugly boils on his back. I told them of my discovery and offered to bring over a half-used tin of "Elmbalm," as it was called, for him to try.

Again, the remedy worked; painlessly and easily it drew out the pus and healed up the boils once the core was out.

Change Your Diet

With this victory under my belt, I became even more zealous than before. One day in a company of people, I was enthusiastically extolling the virtues of my cure for boils when an elderly man looked at me in such a way that I said to him, "What does that look mean?"

"Oh," he replied, "you couldn't bear it; carry on talking!"

"No," I said, "I want you to tell me, even if it hurts!"

"No," he insisted, "it would upset you."

"Go on, tell me. I can take it."

"Okay," he said, "you've asked for it—here it comes! You poor fool! When God made your body, He put enough holes in it to get rid of all the poison without your having to be pockmarked with boils!"

"Go on," I said, "Hit me! I'll take it all!"

"All right," he said. "Let me ask you some questions. Do you like sugar?"

"Yes!"

"Do you like jam?"

"Oh, yes; I like jam and bread, not bread and jam!"

"Cake?"

"Yes!"

"Chocolates?"

"Yes!"

"Well," he said, "there is your trouble: Your blood is all out of order because your diet is all wrong. Alter the balance of your diet, and you will have no more boils! Your boils are an outward sign of an inward condition!"

That was fifty years ago. By dealing with boils I was dealing with the consequences. Since I received that revelation, I have never had another boil!

P-ride. U-nbelief. S-in. Pus! Behind my obvious sin is the unseen pride that produced it. The blood of Jesus is the cleanser for my sin, *not* for my pride! I must *humble myself* under the mighty hand of God. Pride is defined as the treason of the creature against his Creator. Its whole purpose is, like that of Lucifer, to rule and reign in the stead of God. It will die rather than surrender! It copies the whole plan of redemption, which is substitution. *In the stead of.* Christ died *in my stead.* Pride will rule *in God's stead!*

It is *not* just a whim in your hair style, a pardonable extravagance in how you dress or a fond mother's weakness to show how well little Johnny plays the violin. It is a raging monster that would destroy God if it could—a subtle serpent that dresses in a thousand different garbs.

It can weep, it can creep, it can laugh, it can cheer, it can dance, it can mourn. It can preach from the pulpit, sing in the choir, pray in the prayer meeting, vaunt itself in a royal palace or blaspheme drunkenly in a saloon, torture its victims in a dungeon or negotiate with bland charm in an embassy. It speaks all languages and is as much at ease with a whip as with a cocktail. The final indictment is from God Himself: *Everyone* that is proud in heart is an abomination in the sight of God! (Prov. 16:5).

Regarding failure: *You cannot keep your pride and get rid of your sin!* Your problem will break only one way: *pride* (one), *unbelief* (two), *sin* (three). One, two, three; *not* three, two, one. The greater includes the lesser! The lesser does not include the greater. Stop dusting cobwebs and catch the spider!

ELEVEN

LESSONS
LEARNED

I have lived a long time—nearly eighty-five years. In that time, I have made many, many mistakes and experienced much failure. In fact, I have been a great success as a failure. But in my failure, I have learned some things that I am now able to pass on to you. That is the purpose of this book: to impart to you what God, out of His mercy and grace, has taught me.

Failure and Success Must Be Defined by God

First of all, I have learned that failure is not what it

appears to be. It is not, as the Oxford dictionary indicates, a falling short, a breaking down, a coming to nothing or the opposite of success. Failure is a life that leaves God out.

Failure and success must both be defined by God. What appears to be one in our eyes may in fact be the other from God's point of view. Failure may be success and success failure!

Most of us would say that success is the attainment of an object or goal. But true success is not measured by the results we attain; it is measured by our faithfulness. Remember: "That which is highly esteemed among men [status, fame, money, power] is an abomination in the sight of God" (Luke 16:15). *True* success is doing all that we do to the glory of God.

The headiest "wine" man ever drinks is the wine of what the world calls, and what we would think of as, "success"—the pinnacle of greatness. This type of success has to be borne, and if it is not borne to the glory of God, it will bring us down. Tremendous temptations attend those on whom honor and wealth is bestowed. Many people, from all walks of life, have fallen into this category.

William Pitt was appointed Prime Minister of England at the tender age of twenty-one. Elvis Presley and Marilyn Monroe rose quickly to stardom in their day. Neil Armstrong assured himself a place in the history books when he became the first man to set foot on the moon. Numerous athletes have basked in the limelight for a season by distinguishing themselves in sports (400 million people watched Mohammed Ali and Joe Frazier in one of the greatest boxing encounters of all time).

These people and countless others not mentioned were picked from the sea of humanity, for whatever reason, to be exalted above their fellow men. They did not choose their birth or their destiny or their parents. Their lives, some would say, were (or are) lives of success. *Oh, to be a Billy Graham!* sighs the young man as he enters the ministry. He does not realize that success must be borne.

Just as electricity, while a helpful resource, can cause wires to burn too hot and must therefore be regulated in order to be useful, so unseen heavenly power must first be respected by man before it will bless and serve him. Electricity can destroy you or fry your bacon and eggs. Which it does depends on you.

Why is success dangerous? Because it can lead to the rising up of your pride. You may forget, in your hour of success, to whom all credit is really due.

It is God who sovereignly sets us apart and raises us up, not we ourselves. The Word of God reminds us that *all things* come of Him and challenges us to ask ourselves, "Who maketh thee to differ from another? and what hast thou that thou didst not receive? now, if thou didst receive it, why dost thou glory, as if thou hadst not received it?" (1 Cor. 4:7).

Man's glory—pride—is the devil's substitute for God's glory. We must never think we are responsible for our own success, worldly or otherwise. We would do well to heed God's warning to the Israelites:

> Beware that thou forget not the Lord thy God...lest when thou hast eaten and art full, and hast built goodly houses, and dwelt therein; And when thy herds and thy flocks multiply, and thy silver and thy gold is multiplied, and all that thou hast is multiplied; Then thy heart be lifted up, and thou forget the Lord thy God...And thou say in thine heart, *My* power and the might of *mine* hand hath gotten me this wealth (Deut. 8:11-14,17, italics added).

Beware the hour of success, the hour of promotion, the hour when all men speak well of you. Beware! It's dangerous. That's what I've learned, and that's what I've observed.

Living to God

The second thing I have learned from failure is that the only right way to live is to live to God and not to man.

One reason worldly success is so dangerous besides its tendency to lead to pride is that it causes us to live to man rather than to God. We become crowd-pleasers, doing what is expected of us rather than what God tells us to do. Or we work to preserve a false reputation in the eyes of men, thereby living a lie. If you doubt that your behavior reflects a deference to man, try living one day in *absolute truth* with God, your neighbor and yourself. Say and do nothing to man but only to God.

Why do we jump up to dust the furniture or poke the logs in the fireplace when we hear footsteps at the front door? Fair enough, if it's time to clean house or stoke the fire. But if the motive is, "Lest they think I'm lazy...," then we are too concerned about what others think. True humility doesn't mind being thought proud! The "odd" magazine pushed under the cushion and the Bible suddenly opened in "certain" company! The television switched to a different station when the doorbell rings! The sweet voice used with our children and spouse when visitors are present! All of these are examples of living to man.

True success can be defined only in terms of living to God, *not* to man. You cannot serve two masters. To your own Master you stand or fall, and 'twere better to fall to God than to stand to man! It is in your failure that you learn this lesson. Do what you do, to God!

I have a little story that perfectly illustrates the attitude we should have in our hearts about living to God. A very gifted young man had just performed before a packed audience on an electric organ. As the prolonged applause finally died down, a friend said to him, "You must be proud to have all these people cheer you."

"No," the young man replied, "it doesn't move me."

"What!" his friend exclaimed. "You mean this doesn't impress you?"

"No," he responded, "not at all. Come here and I will tell you why. Look up in the balcony. You see that little old man with the bald head? Well, that is my old music teacher. All I ever learned, I learned at his feet. He's forgotten more about music than this whole audience ever knew! One smile from him, one frown from him means more to me than the applause of all this crowd!"

The way we are to live is the way the young organist in the story did: with our eyes on the Man up in the "balcony"! It is His approval that we seek, for only He can define what success and failure truly are. We cannot go wrong if we do whatever we do, to God.

Where Does Human Responsibility Come In?

The third thing I have learned from failure is that when I fail, I must take the responsibility for my mistake. In other words, I must take the blame. If I don't take the blame, I will do it again!

I like to imitate a little boy I knew who, when he was naughty, would never run *from* his daddy but always ran *to* him. He would wrap his arms around Daddy's waist, lay his head on his chest and say, "Sorry, Daddy; sorry, Daddy!"

Have you ever tried to smack a clinging child? Distance lends power to the blow! That's why some boxers get into a clinch. I have learned to agree with my adversary quickly, especially when it is God!

However, once I have admitted that I am at fault, there are three areas in which the sovereignty of God gloves the hand of the responsibility of man: performance, will and choice.

God Has to Change Me

First, performance. I cannot do! *I cannot change myself!* I do not have the ability of myself to stop sinning. If it is to be done, God *must* do it. So He gets the credit because He does the work. And if He doesn't do it, it isn't done!

God Makes Me Willing

Second, will. "It is *God* which worketh in you both *to will* and *to do* of his good pleasure" (Phil. 2:13, italics added). "It is not of him that willeth...but of God" (Rom. 9:16). Whatever God demands, God provides! How often have you heard people say, "You must be willing to leave your sin." But if *you* are willing, then you deserve the glory and thus break the principle of "Thine (that is, God's) is the glory." If He wants the glory, He must do the work!

God will not accept natural willingness which says (like the older brother in the parable), "I will go" and goes not. Admittedly, you must be willing to leave your sin, but He has to work even that in you. And when He does, it will be to will and to work, not of His great misery, but *of His good pleasure.* You will know that He has worked in you because His good pleasure will be your good pleasure. You are to *enjoy* the will of God! *You haven't done the will of God when you have done it miserably.*

Don't insult God by trying from yourself to be willing. God works *in* us both to will and to do of His good pleasure, because it's a divine principle. If the final revelation is "Thine is the glory," then everything must be subject to the governing factor (the glory of God), and nothing will survive except that which is for the glory of God. Therefore, God must do the doing in the doing, or else, He would not have the glory, or the credit, due to His holy name. He must also do the willing in the willing; the Bible declares that. God works in *both* to will and to do of His good pleasure (see Phil. 2:13).

Many people (including me) have sought to make themselves willing. But *God* has to do the work. The hymn-writer wrote: "Deep in unfathomable mines of never-failing skill, He treasures up His bright designs and works his sovereign will." There are depths in me that only God can fathom, where I have had my own "sovereign" will and declared that this, that and the other is "mine."

God has to do a work before I surrender! He may have to send a plague that makes me go whether I want to or not. He may have to put me in a whale's belly or under a cold water faucet. But it is a work that He alone does and therefore when it is done, He alone gets the credit.

I look back on my life now as an old man and realize that I never wanted anything God wanted. I didn't want to get saved, I didn't want to be a preacher, I didn't want to leave home, I didn't want my wife, I didn't want the big house where I live in North Wales, I didn't want to move out when God told me to give up pastoring, I didn't want the kind of life I'm living. But I'm delighted now with everything I've got. And I've discovered something. I don't have to be willing for the will of God. He works it in.

So then, what is left? If God does both the doing in the doing and the willing in the willing, what do I do? Where does human responsibility come in? There are many ways to phrase this question.

Am I a robot? Do I just say, "What is to be, will be?" Am I waiting for God, or is God waiting for me? On which side of the net is the ball? In other words, what will God (in His sovereignty) do that I (in human responsibility) *can't* do, and what will God *not* do that I *must* do?

I Must Choose

These questions bring us to the third area, choice. I have a choice. In fact, the freedom to choose is one of the god-like qualities that separates man from the rest of creation. Everything but man is under compulsion. A caterpillar *must* turn into a butterfly; a tadpole *must* turn into a frog. They don't have any choice about it.

But man was made initially in the image of God, and even though he has now fallen from that image, it's only an evidence that he has the *ability* to fall in his choice. So, while I can make a *wrong* choice, thankfully I can also make a *right* choice.

How do I define my choice? *Lord, I am not willing for Your will, but I choose it; I am willing to be made willing!* I stop fighting Him about the situation and start inviting Him into it. This is man's responsibility. The Bible says, "Choose you this day whom ye will serve" (Josh. 24:15). I *will serve* either God or the devil; sovereignty decrees that. But I do have a choice.

We need to recognize that the spending power of God Almighty is determined by the choice of His children. Psalm 78:41 says, "They [the Israelites]...limited the Holy One of Israel." The Unlimited One may be limited by man's choice. The heart may choose to be a god and rise in pride or humble to God and find grace.

You say, "Aha! If I choose, then I have whereof to glory and thus break the principle that if God wants all the glory (credit), He must do all the work." No! Consider this example.

You are dying of thirst in the desert and God brings you water. He says, "Stoop down and drink and live!" So you stoop down, you drink, you live. Why do you live? "Oh," you answer, "I live because I stooped." Oh, no, you don't! You live because God brought the water. All the stooping in the world would not have saved your life if God had not brought the water. And yet, you would have died if you had not chosen to bend your neck. When God brought the water in sovereignty, you had to stoop in human responsibility in order to preserve your life.

God Fixes the Choice

Thus the blame is all yours if you don't, and the credit is all His if you do. Beware of the philosophy that says, "If the blame is mine, then the credit is mine." Your choice is vital and yet so feeble that God must fix it. We are such fickle creatures!

Our children are a good example of our inconstancy. In the summertime, they're already picking their Christmas presents. But by the time the holiday season rolls around, they've changed their minds a hundred times. You know the scenario.

A boy says to his father, "Dad, buy me a camera for Christmas."

Dad responds, "Look, it's only August. Wait."

September arrives.

"Dad, I don't...I said I wanted a camera, but I don't. I want a bike."

Dad says patiently, "It's just September. Wait and see."

In October, it's something different again.

"Dad, I really want street hockey gear, not a bike."

Dad replies, "It's still too early."

Finally, November comes and goes, and the calendar turns to December, the month of Christmas.

The father says to the son, "Now listen. This time, when you make your choice, that's *it*. I'm fixing it. Now *what do you want?* You can't have them all; you can have one. What is it?"

The child hems and haws, hesitates. "Um, uh, well...."

The father presses. "Well, come on now, what is it?"

In a burst of enthusiasm, the child declares, "A bicycle!"

"Right, that's it. I'll fix it."

So, the son chooses; the father fixes.

We cannot simply decide to turn from our failure and expect to be successful on our own. God must fix the choice for us. Take addiction, for example. People are addicted to everything from television to smoking to food, but even with the best of intentions, they are unable to "give up" their habits without God's grace. "Except the Lord build the house, they labour in vain that build it" (Ps. 127:1). God puts the juice in every orange, and if He doesn't, there is no juice!

The idea of "giving up" or "sacrificing" our sins to God is foolishness, anyway. We need to take our pattern from the birds. They don't sacrifice their plumage to God; they moult. New life from within pushes fresh feathers to the surface and the old ones naturally drop off. We ought to moult for Jesus: Just allow the power of another life to move through and cause the old to drop off. It's a wonderful process.

In measure a young girl may sacrifice her dolls, but in the fullness of time she falls in love, and the power of a greater attraction finally produces a bundle of life called a baby that completely ousts the dead dolls!

I have not played marbles for years, though I did not "give them up" because they were sinful. I put them away because I became a man. Paul says, "When I became a man, I put away childish things" (1 Cor. 13:11). The power of a greater attraction! As the new comes in, the old automatically drops off. I don't mind moulting because *I* don't do it; *God* does it and, as I said before, what God demands, God provides.

So, the credit is God's for the doing in the doing; the credit is God's for the willing in the willing; and the credit is God's for fixing the choice. And yet there's room for human responsibility to operate.

It's somewhat analogous to making a concrete pathway. First you define the path by digging it out with a shovel and edging it with wood boards. Then you pour wet cement into the depression and tamp it and scrape it until it's perfectly smooth. Finally, you cover the path to keep stray cats and mischievous children off until it dries, because you know that in only a few hours it will be set—*fixed*. At that point, only a pick-axe would ever change it.

Our hearts are like the wet cement. Along the pathway of life, there comes (over and over again) a moment of registering, not necessarily with a pen between our fingers, not necessarily on our lips, but in our hearts, whether we will let God be true or not.

We make a choice. When we make the right choice, God "sets the cement"—He fixes it. The words of an old hymn confirm this truth, "Oh, happy day, that fixed my choice, on Thee my Savior and my God." Our choice has to be fixed.

But God meant us to enjoy our wonderful salvation, not just endure it. So He does all the work. He does the doing in the doing, the willing in the willing and the fixing in the choosing.

All we have to do is acknowledge Him in *all* our ways (Prov. 3:6): that is, confide in Him rather than hide from Him; invite Him rather than fight Him. Dare I invite God into my failure and be completely frank and open with Him, having truth ruthlessly with myself? He has promised that if I do, He will direct my paths.

Failure Begins with the Knowledge of Good

The fourth thing I have learned from failure is that it begins with the knowledge of good. The knowledge of good looks like God. One little "o" makes all the difference! Move out of God and into good, and you will soon meet the attendant twin—evil. How good is the knowledge of good when God has forbidden it?

A little bird can be lured out of its cage if someone puts a pencil into the cage and holds it steady. A pencil looks like a perch, so the bird will move off its perch and onto the pencil. Then, in one quick move, the pencil is removed from the cage, and the cage door is shut. The little bird has suddenly lost its abiding place! It is now exposed to all kinds of dangers from the claws of the cat to the clutches of the children.

We leave God, our abiding place, when we move out of God into what is good. We are lured by two "imposters," as the poet Rudyard Kipling called them—triumph and success. Once out of our cages, we are open to the dangers of two other imposters—disaster and failure. But while success takes us out of God, failure can bring us back in.

It may be "good" to pray and "good" to read your Bible (gestures of a "successful" Christian life), but when you trust in these means of grace, then they become a currency to buy grace and you destroy grace as grace. Many things we do are the will of God until we trust in them; then we are on our way into a failure that will reveal to us the evil of our so-called "good."

"I fast twice in the week," said the pompous Pharisee (Luke 18:12). His legalistic adherence to what was considered "good" did not make him righteous before God. It was, instead, the source of his condemnation. "Every one that exalteth himself shall be abased; and he that humbleth himself shall be exalted" (v. 14).

Once we see the root of failure as our understanding, or misunderstanding, of what is good (the pencil instead of the perch!), we immediately see the way out of it: refusing to eat of the tree of the knowledge of good and evil. My refusal to eat helps me to see God in all things. I become one with God when I am one with my circumstances, and that which is good will naturally flow out of the oneness. "And we know that all things work together for good" (Rom. 8:28). A wheel doesn't go around *to become a wheel;* it goes around because *it is a wheel!*

A Positive from the Negative

We have said that failure is not what it appears to be. It is not necessarily the negative we tend to think it is. In fact, it is possible for us to make a positive from the negative, so there is no reason to be negative with the negative.

When a photographer seeks to make a permanent

record of a scene, he aims his camera at it and depresses the shutter release. There is a click and a flash of light, and you have a negative! You may take a look and decide you don't like the negative. Mary, on her wedding day, had a lovely white dress on; but on the negative it is black. You want to tear up the negative, destroy it, discard it. No, don't! Rather, value it; treasure it. Out of it will come the positive result.

When the negative is developed in a dark room in a solution of acid and light is focused on it to shine through it, you obtain a permanent, positive result: a photograph!

In a similar way, failure produces a negative. But when you take it into your dark room and, by faith, focus on it the light you had while in the anointing, you develop a positive, lasting image. Jesus said, "*While ye have light, believe* in the light" (John 12:36, italics added). Revelation is married to situation. What you "see" (revelation) while in the anointing, you make yours in the negative situation by faith.

There is a saying: Give a man a fish, and you feed him for a day; teach a man to fish, and you feed him forever. This saying applies to what I am teaching you about failure: Once you know how to fish, you will never be hungry again. In other words, once you know what to do with your hour of failure, you will never have an hour of failure. Simply bring it into the light of the truth!

The power of the false is in its ability to hide the truth. Failure begins in a lie. Before you sin, you are deceived! As you would look for the sting in a bee, look for the lie in your sin, your failure. That is where it will break. The acid solution of the truth will dissolve it!

My friends, remember this: The actual cause of failure is success! The real danger is the knowledge of good. That's where it all begins. The *fall*—our failure or our sin—is really the *rise*—the point at which we rise up against God! We think we know what is good, we seek to abide in it, we declare ourselves successful (and others unsuccessful) and then we take the credit for what we consider to be "our" success.

Pride is born when man exalts himself. God resists him by withdrawing His grace, and then, as man stands only by grace, all he can do is fall (1 Pet. 5:5). God will not give His glory to another (Is. 48:11). Thus pride is at the back of all the sin and failure in the universe. You won't fall lying on the ground (on your face before God), but you may get dizzy on the roof. If Humpty Dumpty had known he was only an egg, he wouldn't have sat so high up on the wall! The road to *true* success begins when I humble myself to God. *Thine* is the glory! This, my brothers and sisters, is the lost key!

ABOUT THE AUTHOR

Arthur Burt began his preaching career in May 1927 at the tender age of 15. He stood up before an enthusiastic group of about 100 believers at a mission in Newcastle-on-Tyne and gave his testimony. His "sermon" lasted all of five minutes, and when it was over, he couldn't remember anything he had said.

Hardly an auspicious beginning. But then, God didn't call Arthur to be auspicious. He called him to be a living example of the truth of 1 Corinthians 1:26-29: that God has chosen the "foolish things of the world to confound the wise...the weak things of the world to confound the things which are mighty...and things which are not, to bring to nought things that are: That no flesh should glory in his presence."

Born in England in 1912, the only child by his father's second marriage, Arthur was converted at a Sunday evening Baptist service on May 1, 1927, just four weeks before his first speaking engagement. At the time, he had no intention of going into full-time ministry; he just wanted to "get right with God." But God soon made it clear that it was His desire for Arthur to preach.

The Call

At three different meetings attended by thousands of people, evangelist Stephen Jeffries, who did not know

Arthur at all, walked to the front of the platform on which he was speaking, pointed directly at Arthur and said, "Young man, God wants you!"

Initially Arthur resisted, but the call was unmistakeable, and he had no peace until he finally gave in. He joined the Protestant Truth Society and, at age 18, became the youngest preacher ever accepted into their college in London. After graduating from this school in 1930, he was ordained as a Wycliffe Preacher.

Early Days

Equipped with a small travel trailer and a big black horse, Brother Arthur traveled and preached throughout Britain for two years. Then, as a result of his association with some pentecostal friends, he received the baptism in the Holy Spirit with the evidence of speaking in other tongues. Once the Protestant Truth Society got wind of the radical change in him and his theology, he was promptly expelled from the organization.

After pastoring a small church in Huthwaite for a time, Arthur took to the road again, first with the Assemblies of God and then on his own. Later he filled several temporary pastoral roles. Eventually, he accepted a position as the co-pastor of a small church south of London and remained there for 20 years.

In 1940, Arthur married Marjorie Coates, and together, they raised nine children.

A New Appointment

One day, God told Arthur to relinquish his position at the church and move out. Arthur didn't want to go. He fought God on the issue until God threatened to take him home unless he obeyed. When he finally surrendered, God changed his appointment completely and launched him into the ministry he has today.

In the early days he used to go to a church to lead meetings and stay for perhaps a week; now he is sometimes in a different town or city every day. Before he would often preach to large groups of people; now he generally goes to a place to meet with only one person. "It's very different from the way I used to minister," Brother Arthur admits.

"When God changed my appointment, He began to send me all over the world to minister to one person at a time. I've gone to Australia for one man. I've gone to Costa Rica for one man. I've gone to Georgia for one woman. I often end up meeting other people when I go, but initially, God sends me for one person."

Brother Arthur doesn't keep an itinerary. He doesn't live on schedule. From day to day, he seldom knows where he will be next, because he goes where the Father directs him to go and ministers "if He wills." His is an unprogrammed ministry, he claims, that God uses to minister to programmed ministries.

The Man and His Message

Arthur Burt is a man who lives by the principle he discusses in this book: continually giving all the glory to God. The failures he has experienced in his life as a result of living out of himself have made real to him the truth that "in his flesh dwells no good thing" (Rom. 7:18) and have taught him that any good he has ever done in his life is solely to God's credit, not his.

To God's credit, he has done much good. For 70 years, Brother Arthur has ministered throughout Britain and around the world, challenging people of every persuasion to become all that God intends them to be—children who are fully conformed to the image of His Son.

Though he considers himself an evangelist, the real thrust of his message is not salvation, but giving up *all*

116

for Jesus—all of oneself for all of Him. Not many who hear this message are willing to pay the price—total surrender—but to those who are, Brother Arthur offers deep insight and revelation. The truth he imparts, gained from personal experience and an intimate relationship with God, is an inspiration to continually lay down one's own life and take up the life of Christ.

Brother Arthur's message is particularly relevant today as the fire of revival begins to rage in pockets around the world. Arthur believes that this last move of God will bring the baptism of fire prophesied by John the Baptist just before Jesus began His earthly ministry (see Matt. 3:11-12) and that it will usher in what he calls "the day of fullness"—the day in which the children of God will "come in the unity of the faith, and of the knowledge of the Son of God, unto a perfect man, unto the measure of the stature of the fullness of Christ" (Eph.4:13).

Brother Arthur's one-on-one and small group ministry has impacted many lives over the years. His humility and complete dependence on God for direction and provision are a testimony to God's grace and an example for us to follow. His success in "confounding the wise" is an encouragement to us that if we are willing to empty ourselves and allow Christ to live His life through us, we—who are likewise "are nots"—can also bring great glory to God.

The author and his wife maintain their house
for the glory of God and incidentally, to meet man's
need. "I was a stranger and ye took me in!"

If you are interested in obtaining further information
about their ministry, write or call the author at
the following address and phone number:

Arthur W. Burt
Bron Wendon
Conway Road
Penmaenmawr
Gwynedd, North Wales
Phone: 0149-262-3338

"The glory of this latter house shall be greater
than of the former, saith the Lord of hosts: and in
this place will I give peace, saith the Lord of hosts."
Haggai 2:9

Businessmen will invest their money where
there are prospects of rich dividends for their
capital. God will invest His grace in human lives
where there will be dividends to the glory of His
great name! We are stewards of this grace which
came with truth by Jesus Christ (John 1:17).

What are we to do with it?
Read 1 Samuel 22:1-2 and Luke 10.

Christ is the answer to every problem
of our sin-sick civilization.

If you enjoyed reading *Surrender,* we would like to recommend the following books:

The Prophetic Romance
by Fuchsia Pickett
In *The Prophetic Romance* Fuchsia Pickett unlocks a hidden truth--a fresh revelation for the last days. With profound biblical insight from the Holy Spirit, she shows how the book of Ruth is more than a courtship between two lovers. It foreshadows the coming of Jesus and the restoration of the church.

Receiving Divine Revelation
by Fuchsia Pickett
Learn how to read *out* of Scripture what God intended rather than reading *into* it from your own cultural and denominational background. One of today's leading Bible scholars shows you how. In this book, Fuchsia Pickett describes how you can receive divine revelation by relying on the Holy Spirit to guide your study of God's Word. Following her instruction will turn your devotional time into an opportunity to truly discern the voice of the Lord.

Available at your local Christian bookstore or from:

Creation House
600 Rinehart Rd.
Lake Mary, FL 32746
Phone: 407-333-3132
Fax: 407-333-7100
Web site: http:www//creationhouse.com